The Friendship Book

_____

TO

_____

FROM

_____

DATE

_____

OCCASION

What Christian leaders
are saying ...

"I have had the pleasure of knowing Steve Wingfield for 30 years. No one that I know is better qualified to write a book about friendship. Steve helps you discover the power and purpose of building and maintaining true friendship. *The Friendship Book* is a must read!"

Dr. John Maxwell, Author, President of
Injoy and chairman of *Global Pastors Network*

"Our Lord has created all of us to live in loving and meaningful relationships with him and with others. . . . I thank God for the privilege of enjoying wonderful friendships with many Christian brothers and sisters. . . . I thank God for Steve's friendship and for his significant ministry."

Dr. Paul Cedar, Chairman, Mission America

"Steve Wingfield has written autobiographically as he is a personification of the type of friend reflected in *The Friendship Book*. Steve is a man who has built his life around sharing Christ, the greatest friend of all, with all those he meets and has typified for me what true friendship is—someone selflessly giving himself or herself in obedience to God's command to those whom he or she finds in the footsteps of life. Steve has produced a creative work portraying the true qualities of friendship, its dangers and results, and the fulfillment of our human nature by being a friend to those in need, whether deserving or not."

Tom Philips, Vice President of Crusades and Training,
Billy Graham Evangelistic Association

"No one could write a better book on friendship than Steve Wingfield. He personifies the nature of friendship. He has been my friend, and I could not ask for a greater friend. Steve phones me long distance every Sunday morning and together we pray, discuss our ministries and enjoy fellowshipping together. May you use the lessons of *The Friendship Book* to reach others, as Steve was reached for Christ through friends, and as he has reached out to touch many lives."

Dr. Elmer L. Towns, Author and Co-Founder of Liberty University

"There is a language that comes to us through friends. One of the treasured gifts of God in life is the gift of friendship. This gift comes as His grace because I have seen it manifested even when the recipient is undeserving. Over the years as I have traveled and sat at a meal with people around the world, I have carried away with me this beautiful gift. On every continent I have memories, enriched beyond measure, of some friend who at some time shared with me the gift of hospitality. When feelings are down and the road seems desolate, it is the friend who carries you along."

Dr. Ravi Zacharias, President, Ravi Zacharias International Ministries

"Too often today, men walk through life with no one who will love them enough to challenge them when they are settling for the mediocre or correct them when they are wrong. . . . Thank you Steve for reminding us of the importance of friendship in our lives and how we can best glorify God in the relationships He has given us here on earth."

Dr. Bob Reccord, President,
North American Mission Board, Southern Baptist Convention

"Steve Wingfield is a true friend indeed. His new book on friendship speaks to the heart. He reminds us all of the value of lasting friendships and what they mean to our lives, our families and our ministries."

Dr. Jerry Falwell, Founder and Chancellor, Liberty University

"Friends that are true friends are rare and precious. Anything that is rare and precious needs to be carefully maintained. Proverbs 18:24 says, 'A man of many friends will come to ruin' (NAS)."

Dr. Adrian Rogers, Pastor, Bellevue Baptist Church

"Friendship is a God given gift, and God alone who made hearts can unite people in true friendships. [Steve,] the respect I have for your ministry has contributed to my desire to be your friend. . . . Our respective ministries remind me of two hands of the Gospel. One, the preaching of the Word and evangelism; and the other, . . . healing the sick and meeting human needs through giving a cup of water in the name of the Lord."

Bob Pagett, President, Assist International

"Some friendships don't need daily contact to stay alive. When you see some friends once a year, or once every three years, after an hour of updates your relationship picks up right where you left off. These are relationships of trust, respect, compatibility and values that are in alignment. This is what describes our friendship. . . . Steve, thanks for being my friend."

Bobb Biehl, President, Master Planning Inc.

"Steve and I have been friends for about 20 years. . . . I always feel refreshed and encouraged to be all God wants of me after I have spent time with Steve."

Ben S. Beiler, Founding President, Beiler-Campbell Realtors
Board of Directors, Steve Wingfield Evangelistic Association

"Friendship is a little bit like my definition of ministry: '90% of ministry is showing up.' Steve, 90% of my friendship with you is that you show up. Even when we're far apart, I know that you are there for me. If I would ever be in trouble physically, financially or God forbid, morally, I know I could call on you. That's a true friend. Plus, you're a blast to be with, whether serious ministry or just goofing off."

Rev. John Schmid, Common Ground Prison Ministries

"Occasionally, someone comes across your path, and you immediately connect with them. Your heart beats with the same passion. Your minds travel down the same road. Your eyes see the same vision. In one moment, a friendship is born. That happened when I met Steve Wingfield. It wasn't a short-term friendship. It's one that has lasted for years. I'll always be thankful to God for bringing Steve across my path."

Rev. Sammy Tippit, President, Sammy Tippit Ministries

"Friendship . . . is nurtured in mutual respect and cultivated in honesty and integrity. It is not bound by time, space or location. It dispels envy and jealously. . . . It grows best in the soil of sacrifice and servanthood. . . . Most people live their lives and never encounter the lasting fragrance of a mutual friendship. I am happy to say that my friendship with Steve began to blossom on the day we met and has continued to be a source of joy and encouragement ever since."

Rev. Jerry Drace, Evangelist

"It has been said of some evangelists, 'How they love people and hate persons,' meaning that it is difficult to get next to them. This is not so of Steve. . . . He has his work rooted in the church and shares meaningfully in congregational life as an expression of his caring spirit. . . . Thank God for the gift of friendship, of giving and receiving in the spirit of Christ."

Dr. Myron S. Augsburger, Author and Evangelist

The
Friendship
Book

The Friendship Book

STEVE WINGFIELD
with Michelle L. W. Curlin

world
PUBLISHING
SINCE 1928

This book is dedicated to my family and friends. To Mom and Dad, who modeled for me the art of friendship. To my wife, Barbara: For the past 30 years you have exhibited the loyalty and commitment needed for meaningful friendship. You have made our home a loving haven. To my children, Michelle and her husband Howard, David and his wife Havilah: I thank God for you daily. I am proud of you, for there is "no greater joy than to hear that my children are walking in the truth" (3 John 4). To the Board of Directors of the Steve Wingfield Evangelistic Association: Thank you for your prayers, support and commitment. You are my friends and partners in evangelism. To the ministry team: I thank God for bringing us together. Thank you for believing in the dream and serving to reach a new generation for Christ. Many people have modeled for me the principles found in this book. I thank God for your investments in my life.

Published by World Publishing, Nashville, TN 37214
www.worldpublishing.com

Table of Contents

Acknowledgments

Michelle, you are not only a wonderful daughter and mother of my first grandchild, Phin, but also I am indebted to you for your tireless effort on this book. Thank you for asking thought-provoking questions and sticking to the task. You have taken what I wrote and made it much better. Barbara, you are a great and honest proofreader. Bruce Barbour and the team at World Publishing, thanks for bringing this passion of mine into print. Jerry Brecheisen, thank you for birthing the vision for this book. To others who have read this manuscript, thank you for your input and feedback. You have sharpened my message.

All Scripture quotations are from the New International Version, unless otherwise indicated.

Foreword

Years ago, Dale Carnegie wrote *How to Win Friends and Influence People*. Not surprisingly, this motivating book became a runaway bestseller, helping millions of people develop winning ways of success in public relations. There is no doubt that respect and influence come with making friends.

Valid as are Carnegie's principles, Steve Wingfield takes friendship to a higher level in *The Friendship Book*. His concern is not that we receive greater popular recognition or gain our end in business. Steve walks us through the art of developing relationships that have eternal value, friendships that lead to a personal experience with Jesus Christ.

Using the Bible as his guide, Steve shows how we make such friends. It's a way of life everyone can follow. Nothing about the teaching is abstract or theoretical. With captivating simplicity, he covers the practical issues of cultivating positive impressions with people, an area where most of us need more sensitivity.

Steve illustrates truth out of his own ministry experience. As few persons I know, Steve's loving lifestyle exemplifies what he teaches. Little wonder that he has become one of the most effective evangelists of this generation.

I plan to get a copy of *The Friendship Book* for all my children to read. This is the kind of realistic, easy-to-understand admonition they will appreciate, and I believe it will also be a blessing to you.

Dr. Robert B. Coleman
Distinguished Professor of Evangelism
Gorden Conwell Theological Seminary
Author, *The Master Plan of Evangelism*

Making Friends

"Friendship is one of the sweetest joys of life. Many might have failed beneath the bitterness of their trials had they not found a friend."

CHARLES SPURGEON

"Wishing to be friends is quick work, but friendship is slow-ripening fruit."

ARISTOTLE

I bought my first car when I was 15, with a fresh driver's license in my wallet. Dale, Edward and I went in on the deal together. It was a '49 Plymouth; the driver's side door tied shut with chicken wire. Together, we shelled out 75 dollars. What a deal! That piece of junk made some great memories. In the winter, we took turns sledding behind it. The rest of the year, we drove it just about everywhere, including off-roading through the swamps of Eastern Virginia where it met its final demise. I would not recommend such reckless behavior, but it sure was fun!

I have a friend who loves antique cars. He would probably see a lot more potential in that '49 Plymouth than my buddies and I ever considered. When someone mentions antique cars, he starts listening with a new level of interest. Antique cars are his passion.

If you have ever been to an antique auto show, you know that only half of the enjoyment comes from walking up and down the rows of gleaming cars, admiring the various makes and models on display. The other half comes from talking with the owners.

Perhaps you've seen the way they rush out after a rain shower to carefully wipe down their prized possessions with an expensive chamois. Have you watched an owner hover hawk-like over sticky-fingered children who wander too close to sparkling fenders and chrome? Yet, if you linger over a certain model and ask a few questions, you may be surprised. These protective collectors are all too willing to whip out their scrap-books. They'll gladly recount the history of their meticulously restored automobiles.

Seeing through the rust and dents

As you study the "before and after" photographs of those auto-mobiles, you can only wonder what these artisans saw in the original relics. Most of their "discoveries" were made in dilapi-dated barns or overgrown junkyards. What enabled them to see through the rust, dents and rotting tires to the unique structure underneath? At what point did the project turn from salvaging an old heap to creating a work of art?

They will tell you that it all has to do with love and hard work. That pile of metal peering out from beneath a greasy tarp evoked a memory from childhood, a spark of something that thrilled them. Soon, the process of restoration turned to bonding.

The collector also realizes that restoration isn't the only goal. He has to keep his auto in mint condition with regular mainte-nance. What would be the point of restoring and maintaining a beautiful automobile, if not to drive it or showcase it for oth-ers to appreciate?

Making friends

Friendship is a lot like the process of restoring a classic car.

1. *Friendship isn't something that "just happens."* It's hard, sweaty work. Sure, the spark that initiates the relationship may be based on a circumstance, but the bonding occurs over time. You invest thought, energy and conversation. You commit to relationship. Then you begin to recognize something special in that person. You discover that you share a unique perspective, an understanding of one another. You are comfortable together. You trust each other with your deepest concerns.

2. *Friendship is restorative.* A true friend sees not only who a person is but who that person can be. Friendship sees the possibilities rather than the problems. It looks for the diamonds, even diamonds in the rough. Friendship sees the potential in others and works to create an atmosphere of acceptance where that promise can blossom. It looks beyond flaws and failures, for the higher purpose of being friends.

3. *Friendship is maintenance-oriented.* It commits itself to words and actions that will strengthen the bond. It keeps the relationship in good working order, avoiding jealousy or taking each other for granted. Friendship "showcases" the relationship at every opportunity, treating each person as special, even including others in its celebration.

You may be thinking, *That sounds great, but I've never seen a friendship like that!* Let me introduce you to my Lord and Friend, Jesus Christ. Perhaps you already know him. But have you ever learned from him what it means to be a friend?

Jesus raises the bar for friendship. His model for human relationships can change your life. I like to call Jesus' model, "purposeful friendship."

Purposeful friendship

∞

"Purposeful friendship" extends a hand beyond those with whom we have a natural affinity to include those outside our parameters. It helps us see through peculiarities and pretenses to the unique individuals God created around us. Purposeful friendship takes everyday social interaction to the next level. It fosters friendships of substance, not dependent on circumstances. Grounded in a personal relationship with God, we are freed to love people with confidence and abandon.

Purposeful friendship sees as God sees: each of us are

handcrafted, gifted, valuable and created for a purpose. "'Love the Lord your God with all your heart and with all your soul and with all your mind and with all your strength . . . Love your neighbor as yourself'" (Mark 12:30–31). Purposeful friendship restores love to its original design. It's not merely a feeling, but an action: "Let us not love with words or tongue but with actions and in truth" (1 John 3:17–19).

I invite you to join me in discovering, restoring and maintaining purposeful friendships.

> *"We cannot tell the precise moment when friendship is formed. As in filling a vessel drop by drop, there is at last a drop which makes it run over; so in a series of kindnesses there is at last one which makes the heart run over."*
>
> JAMES BOSWELL

> *"Friendship is the greatest enrichment that I have found."*
>
> ADLAI STEVENSON

Friendship Redefined

"Do to others as you would have them do to you."

Jesus, Luke 6:31

"What makes the Dead Sea dead? It is all the time receiving, but never giving out anything. Why is it so many friendships grow cold? Perhaps it is because they too are all the time receiving, never giving."

Dwight L. Moody

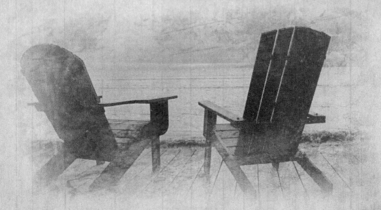

We are a society obsessed with impressing and interacting with others. Daytime television talk show guests describe relationship issues, and "experts" offer instant answers to long-term problems. Books on relationships regularly hit bestseller lists. Pop magazines chronicle the rise and fall of alliances among the rich and famous. Internet sites feature personal ads and chat rooms where people can interact with others and discuss relationships. Late night infomercials market tapes and seminars on developing winsome ways.

Yet, many of us are starved for meaningful friendship. Loneliness is a significant problem in our society. According to Barna Research, almost one third of Americans acknowledge that they're "trying to find a few good friends." In the irony of the computer age, the more we get connected, the more isolated we become. More of our jobs are being transferred across the country, away from extended family. We're too busy to get to know our neighbors. Many of our elderly spend their last days in institutions far from home. Divorce has wracked the security of home with aching loneliness for countless spouses and children. As the Beatles crooned in their song, *Eleanor Rigby*, "All those lonely people . . . where do they all come from?"

Where's the disconnection between our obsession with successful relationships and the bleak reality? Is our "need" for friendship a sign of weakness? What exactly is friendship, anyway?

When I think of friendship, I remember a surprising reunion I witnessed the summer I was twelve. I was hoeing in the garden with my dad behind our home in the rural town of Amherst, Virginia. As we were working, I looked up to see a man coming toward us, walking slowly down the hill from our house. He was carrying a movie camera, quite a sight in those days for Amherst. My dad glanced up and I asked, "Do you know him?"

The man paused and called to my father, "Floyd!"

My dad dropped the hoe and ran to meet him, brushing the dirt off his hands. "Jim!" he cried in surprise. The two men embraced like old friends.

As I later learned, my dad had long been reaching out to Jim in friendship. Jim lived with his family in our town for many years. He was a rough man who kept falling back into alcoholism. My parents, on a tight budget of their own, had often shared groceries with Jim's wife and children.

One Sunday morning when I was a baby, our family passed Jim on the way to church. He was drunk, lying passed out in a ditch along the road. Dad took our family to church and returned to get Jim. He hauled him into the car and drove him to our home where he bathed and fed him. Dad then put him in bed and told him, "Jim, you do not have to live like this! Jesus can set you free and bring meaning to your life."

Jim soon returned to the bottle and his old habits. Eventually, he abandoned his wife and children and moved to California. Despite his best distractions or achievements, there was one thing he could not shake: the memory of my dad's friendship. He later told Dad, "Your friendship was the Hound of Heaven that kept pursuing me. I couldn't forget it. Finally, I had to give my life up to Jesus and seek his forgiveness."

Jim returned to Virginia to be reunited with his wife and children. He then determined to find my dad to thank him for his persistent friendship.

That may not be the kind of story that first springs to your mind when you think of friendship. In some ways, it's not my preferred method of making friends either. But friendship isn't just about "hanging out" and sharing the "warm fuzzies" with people who are like us. Friendship can be demanding. It requires vision and persistence. You may not be reaching out to an addict every time, but I can guarantee you that your friends will be imperfect. Through the messiness of our everyday inter-actions, I believe that God has an amazing plan for our relation-ships. Friendship is meant to change lives.

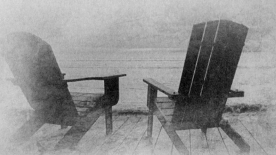

Jesus redefines friendship

When Jesus Christ arrived on earth, God in the flesh, he changed a lot of things—including friendship. Jesus modeled a picture of human relationships that the world had only caught glimpses of since the Garden of Eden. He raised the bar for friendship. In his words and example, he calls us to a radical kind of friendship that is the very thing we have been craving all along.

Jesus was asked, "Which is the greatest commandment?" He answered,

> "'Love the Lord your God with all your heart and with all your soul and with all your mind.' This is the first and greatest commandment. And the second is like it: 'Love your neighbor as yourself.'"
>
> Matthew 22:37–39

How do we demonstrate love for God? By loving the people around us. That is a call to radical friendship. "For anyone who does not love his brother, whom he has seen, cannot love God, whom he has not seen" (1 John 4:20). In other words, people who have accepted Jesus' call should be the best friends this world has ever known. Our love for God fuels our love for others. Our passion for God is authenticated in our everyday acts of friendship.

Born to be friends

Friendship is not something that must be contrived. We were created by God to be friends. As surely as we are born with the natural tendency to rebel against God, we are also born with a desire to have a relationship with him. We are incomplete spiritually unless we are reconciled to our Creator. That divine friendship factor affects all of our earthly relationships.

Mister Rogers, the affable children's television host sang, "Won't you be my neighbor?" That strikes a chord in our spirits. His musical message was: "Won't you be my friend?" The response from young and old alike is a resounding "Yes!" We are not born to be social hermits, to live apart from others. We are designed not for caves, but for community. Because God's friendship love flows through our spiritual veins, we have a deep-down craving for a "kindred spirit."

Christ's love in us

Jesus has raised the bar for friendship: love your neighbor like you love yourself (Matthew 22:39, my paraphrase). Look out for my colleague like I look out for my

own interests? Take care of my friend like I take care of myself? Those are tall orders. How can we live like that?

When we live in right relationship with Christ, he empowers us to love others with his love. When his love is released in us, our acceptance of others will not be based on what they have accumulated or accomplished. Christ's love accepts others, recognizing that they too are created and loved by God. "Man looks at the outward appearance, but the LORD looks at the heart" (1 Samuel 16:7). When God's love is released, we will not turn aside because of a person's age, status or ethnic background. We open our lives and hearts because Christ's love fuels a consuming passion for friendship and community.

God showed me how to see people the way he does through the example of a seven-year-old boy. The first year of our marriage, Barbara and I lived in an upstairs apartment of an old house in Salem, Virginia. Our friends John and Connie Swartz lived on the first floor with their two sons. Johnny was seven and Kent was five.

One summer afternoon John and I were sitting on the front porch talking and enjoying ice-cold glasses of sweet tea. (If you are from north of the Mason-Dixon Line, you may not know the importance of the *sweet* tea Southern tradition.) Johnny and Kent were playing in the yard with four neighbor boys. When the other boys left for their homes, John's sons joined us on the porch. Johnny began telling us about one of the boys, but his dad and I couldn't understand about which of the boys

Johnny was talking. Finally, a bit exasperated, Johnny said, "He's the one with the red bike!"

Only then did I realize whom Johnny was trying to describe. The young boy with the red bike was the only African-American among the boys who had been playing together. But Johnny did not see skin color, he saw a friend with a red bike. I prayed at that moment that God would give me such eyes.

Friendship among God's people

A few years ago, I was standing in the foyer of a church on Sunday morning as the pastor and his wife greeted people arriving for the service. A middle-aged woman smiled as she approached. "I look forward to Sunday mornings!" she told them. "Because these are the only two hugs I get all week."

Wow. That is both a hopeful and a disappointing picture in light of Christ's plan for friendship among his people. How encouraging that this single woman could count on getting hugs and a warm welcome on Sunday morning. That's a reflection of Christ's love in us, reaching out with love and acceptance, made tangible in a hug.

Yet, God intended his people to live in relationship throughout the week. We're not meant to save

meaningful interaction for Sunday morning. God gave us friendships to show his love for us far beyond the church walls. Friends give life to God's love through phone calls, visits and time spent together.

Meaningful friendship is all too rare in our society and in our churches. Living in our little sanitized worlds, many of us are isolated, segregated and lonely. But we have reason to be encouraged. Jesus has redefined friendship. He has modeled it for us, and offers the power of his love to make it happen. Are you getting a vision for the kind of friendship God desires for you? It can bring meaning and fulfillment to your most casual relationships. It can change your life.

One of my favorite verses is Philippians 1:6. As we look into God's plan for friendship, I am praying for you, "being confident of this, that he who began a good work in you will carry it on to completion until the day of Christ Jesus."

> *"Is any pleasure on earth as great as a circle of Christian friends by a fire?"*
>
> C. S. LEWIS

> *"Friendship may be hard to precisely define, but it is easy to recognize."*
>
> DAVID L. SHANK

The Source of Friendship

"Oh, for the days when I was in my prime, when God's intimate friendship blessed my house . . ."

JOB 29:4

"He is your friend who pushes you nearer to God."

ABRAHAM KUYPER

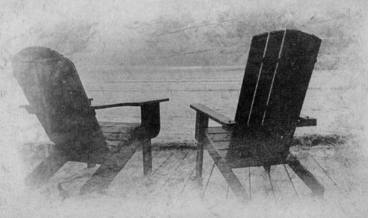

In the popular Mitford novels, author Jan Karon chronicles the lives of an Episcopalian priest and the quirky characters of Mitford, North Carolina. In an interview recorded in her book, *Out of Canaan*, Karon responds to a reader's observation that Father Tim always seems to be "in the thick of things whether he wants to be or not." Karon explains that this enables the reader "to see far more of Father Tim's humanity because he is surrounded by people. That means his heart is going to be broken and his patience is going to be stretched— all of the things that happen when we get involved with other people."

In the beginning . . .

From the beginning of time, God has chosen to get "into the thick of things" with humanity. Your intrinsic need to relate to others is not an anomaly. Relationship is built into human nature by God's design. At the very birthplace of humanity, God lovingly declared, "It is not good for the man to be alone"

(Genesis 2:18). We were never meant to operate in isolation. This aligns with another pivotal statement even earlier in the Bible. God says, "Let *us* make man in *our* image, in *our* likeness" (1:26, emphasis mine). Inherent in our design is the image of God: the God of relationship. In this image is the "spiritual DNA" of relationships. We are marked with the very essence of God's nature. In his book, *Right Relationships,* Tom Marshall calls God a "God of relationships, a Trinity, an eternal society of Father, Son and Holy Spirit, one God."

Before God created us, He was already a God of communication.

- He spoke the world into existence: "And God said . . ." (Genesis 1).
- God dialogued internally concerning the decision to make mankind: "Let us make . . ." (Genesis 1:26).
- He then initiated dialogue with humanity: "God blessed them and *said to them,* 'Be fruitful and increase in number'"(Genesis 1:28, emphasis mine).

The God of love

God is full and complete in himself. Creating humanity was not something he had to do. God does not need our confirmation to prove his existence. Although we need God in every aspect of our being, he does not *need* us at all. Yet, God is the God of relationships.

Why did he bother? Why complicate things? He is God, after all. As God, he is self-sufficient. He is all knowing. Even before he made us, he knew we'd let him down. He knew we would forget to thank him, that we would take him for granted, and that we would sometimes turn our backs on him. Why would Almighty God open himself to something that Scripture says broke his heart? Only several generations after creating Adam and Eve, God saw so much evil in humanity that he "was grieved that he had made man on the earth, and his heart was filled with pain" (Genesis 6:6).

Why did God bother? He bothered because he is the God of love (1 John 4:8). Everything he causes or allows in our lives comes from his loving purpose for us and his desire to be glorified in us. Love expresses itself best in relationship. Our love for God may be largely based on need. However, God's love for us is what scholar C. S. Lewis describes in his book *The Four Loves* as "gift-love," an unconditional outpouring and overflowing of God's divine nature. Many people's first worship experience centers on hearing the words, "For God so loved the world that he gave . . ." (John 3:16).

God's unconditional love is the source of friendship.

Our affinity toward others is from him. Our respect for others comes from him. Our love for others comes from him. Our acceptance and affirmation of others comes from him. Our acts of service for others come from him. *He is the Source.*

God's 3-dimensional design

Did you realize that God's unconditional love for us is the impetus for our human interactions and the model for building meaningful friendships? Have you thought of a relationship with the God of all creation in that way?

We generally hear about a two-dimensional love between God and us: God loves us, and we are to love him. But that's only part of the design. Like golden threads, we are woven into the fabric of God's unconditional love. His love is alive—moving, working, renewing—in us, around us and through us. It's three-dimensional. God loves us. He models love for us and loves others through us. He even loves us through people he places in our lives.

God's personal relationship with us is the catalyst behind our friendships with others. It is the standard to test our interactions with one another. It is the pattern by which we may discern our motives for friendship.

God created us, and he loves his creation. We are not an afterthought. God knew us even before he formed the earth (Ephesians 1:4). We are his plan, and he desires to live in relationship with us. He created us in community because he desires that we also live in relationship with people.

Part of God's design for the complex interactions of our world is the inherent individuality of each tree, each worm and every person. God's unconditional love endows us with individuality. He handcrafts every human life (Psalm 139:14–16). As individuals, we are custom-made. We are unique, one of a kind. There are more than six billion people on planet earth and no one else is like you. Just as each falling snowflake has a totally unique design, so God has designed humanity with stand-alone attributes. You have your own fingerprint, your own DNA. God created you uniquely you, and that makes you an irreplaceable friend.

God is not interested in crafting tiny ivory pawns placed in rows on a chessboard. His idea of individuality does not mean we are assigned to little squares and permitted to function only within tight parameters. His unconditional love is "gift-love." He does not constrain us to respond to him. By creating us uniquely and giving us free will, God makes it clear that he wants a relationship, a purposeful "two-way" interaction. By placing us in families, communities and relationships, God demonstrates that he wants our relationships to be three-dimensional: drawing from himself, the Source, and relating to others in love.

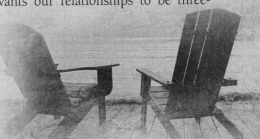

God's loving-kindness

The scriptural expression "loving-kindness" epitomizes God's quality of getting into "the thick of things" with us. God told the prophet Jeremiah, "I have loved you with an everlasting love; I have drawn you with loving-kindness" (Jeremiah 31:3). Like sacrifice, protection, and discipline, God's loving-kindness is one of the ways he shows love to his children.

God's loving-kindness is found in companionship and covenant. In the beginning of time, we find him "walking in the garden in the cool of the day" (Genesis 3:8). There's an easygoing, almost casual tone to those words, as if God was in the habit of taking an evening stroll in the Garden of Eden, coming down to our turf and actively seeking companionship. With Old Testament men like Noah, Abraham and Moses, God's loving-kindness took on the deeper implications of covenant. He honored them as partners in that most significant kind of relationship. God declared to the Israelites in the wilderness, "Know therefore that the LORD your God, he is God, the faithful God, who keeps his covenant and his *loving-kindness* to a thousandth generation with those who love him and keep his commandments" (Deuteronomy 7:9, italics mine, NAS). But they did not always keep their end of the bargain.

Jesus lived out God's loving-kindness in the most people-saturated ministry the world has known. Yet, even those closest to him turned their backs on the blessings of his loving commitment to them. Jesus' apostles each turned from him at the time of his betrayal and arrest. Even his own brother, James, misunderstood his cause and distanced himself from Jesus.

We cannot say the same for God. He always keeps his "end of the bargain."

Faithfully.

Consistently.

Lovingly.

Again in the Mitford series, Karon's novel *A Light in the Window* finds Father Tim taking in a freckle-faced, cow-licked, rough-around-the-edges boy named Dooley. Never married and nearing retirement, Father Tim feels complete bewilderment as Dooley turns the rectory upside down with his raucous behavior and peculiar worldview. But eventually Dooley settles down and becomes like a son to him. "One of the best things he had ever done was bring Dooley Barlowe home." Father Tim muses, "Yes, he'd been trouble and calamity and plenty of it, but worth it and then some."

That's the other thing about God's unconditional lovingkindness. He genuinely likes us. In fact, Scripture tells us that he delights in us. "The Lord will again

delight in you and make you prosperous, just as he delighted in your fathers" (Deuteronomy 30:9). He enjoys getting into the thick of it with us. He delights to be with us in times of tears and times of triumph. He has promised to walk with us through the valleys and along the mountain peaks of life (Psalm 23, 18). It is that kind of security and safety that gives us freedom to reach out to others with Jesus' kind of friendship.

I was pastor at a church in Roanoke, Virginia, in the mid 1970's when Doug came to church. He was the kind of guy that can't keep a low profile. As a soldier in Vietnam, he had lost both his legs at the hip when he stepped on a landmine. Since then, Doug had been living the hippie lifestyle in a remote mountain cabin in Southern Virginia, high on drugs and alcohol. His sandy red hair and beard were long and wild. His wife had taken their two children and moved to Florida.

Roy, a burly tattooed man with a thick Southern twang, was a new believer at our church. A couple days each week, Roy would leave his construction work a little early to go tell people about Jesus. That's how he found Doug. Two more opposite characters could not have met. But Roy shared the good news about Jesus with Doug and led him in prayer. He then invited Doug to come to church on Sunday.

When Roy returned home, he called to tell me about Doug.

"Is it okay if he comes to church?" he asked.

"Of course, it's okay, Roy!" I responded. "Anybody is welcome at our church."

"But Pastor Steve, this guy is *wild!*" Roy warned me.

"That's fine. If he's not welcome, I'll leave with him." I said.

The following Sunday morning, I was standing on the platform, singing the first hymn when Doug rolled into the sanctuary. Roy had underestimated the situation. This guy looked a lot like the cartoon character, Yosemite Sam. Doug was wearing a flannel shirt and bib overalls with the craziest reddish hair I'd ever seen.

Doug rolled up the center aisle and stopped beside the fifth row from the front. He grasped the arm of the wooden pew and hoisted himself into the seat. He crossed his arms and sat with his chin lifted, daring anyone to approach him. By now every eye in the place was on Doug.

He hadn't been seated in the pew more than a minute, when a prim gray-headed lady rose from her seat across the auditorium. Mrs. Zula Grub picked up her purse, slid out of her pew, crossed the aisle and walked right up to Doug. Stepping around his wheelchair, Mrs. Grub leaned down, kissed him on the cheek and said, "I'm glad you're here. May I sit with you?"

Talk about God's loving-kindness! He delivers it in the most amazing ways. Doug later told me that he had come to church just waiting for someone to tell him to cut
his hair or clean up
his act. He was ready
to spring for the door.

The only thing he wasn't prepared for happened. He said, "Everybody loved me and it freaked me out!"

As soon as I gave an invitation to respond at the conclusion of the Sunday morning service, Doug hoisted himself back into his wheelchair and rolled straight to the front. He slid out of his chair and fell on his face in front of the altar. I doubt there was a dry eye in the place as Doug gave up his life to Christ. That year, God's loving-kindness sent reverberations through the Bent Mountain hippies.

Doug came back to church Sunday night, and after my message, he asked if he could say a few words. He rolled up to the front and Roy and another man lifted his wheelchair onto the platform. Through tears, Doug tried to express the great joy he had experienced in giving his life to Christ. He was overwhelmed to be received and accepted with open arms and unconditional love by the church family. I can still hear him say, "I don't deserve any of this, but it is so good to be forgiven and accepted."

Doug then shared with us that he had a wife and two children who had left him and moved back to Florida. He said, "I am driving to Florida tonight. I am going to ask them to forgive me and come home with me. Will you pray for me?"

Our church family gathered around Doug sitting in his wheelchair. We laid hands on him and prayed for him. He left the service and drove all night to St. Petersburg. Susan and their two small children returned to Bent Mountain with Doug.

The following Saturday, Roy got a call from Doug at midnight. Doug said, "Roy, we have a house full of our friends, and I've told them all I know about Jesus. Could you come up here and tell them what you know?" Roy drove up to Bent Mountain and found a house filled with hippies who were smoking dope and wanted to learn more about Jesus. He stayed with them until 2 A.M. and encouraged them to come to church later that morning.

When the service began on Sunday, the back two rows were filled with hippies from Bent Mountain. The strong scent of pot hung in the sanctuary. At the conclusion of the message, I gave an invitation and the back two rows emptied as all the hippies responded to the call of Christ. On Sunday night, the crew from Bent Mountain was back. They moved from the back row to the front row and began to grow in their new-found faith in Christ.

Through faith, we are offspring of the very Father of friendship. We are born again to love. To accept. To give. To extend our hearts and hands to others. Born to live beyond social strata, free of boundaries. Born again to see lives changed through Jesus' radical friendship.

God walked in the garden "in the cool of the day." He went looking for a friend.

Someone to love.

Someone to enjoy.

Someone to accept.

Someone to affirm.

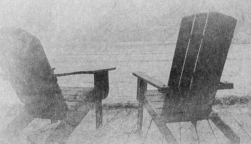

God initiated friendship. His Son, Jesus, furthered the relationship, becoming God-in-the-flesh and leaving his footsteps in the dust alongside the men and women he called "friends."

The God who invented friendship is also the Source of friendship. "Every good and perfect gift" really does come from our loving Father in heaven (James 1:17). Friendship is no exception. God has invested so much in you already. He has given you the desire for meaningful friendship and he wants to fulfill that desire.

> *"True happiness consists not in the multitude of friends, but in the worth and choice."*
>
> BEN JONSON

> *"I have been thinking about God's friendship, walking in the garden in the cool of the day (Genesis 3). What an expression of His love! In His Friendship, He wanted to be close. . . . Despite our failure He reached out to us. . . . He met the demands of justice with His mercy. Friendship gave all. This is supreme, indeed unfathomable, friendship."*
>
> ALAN ARMSTRONG

Jesus Calls Us "Friends"

"Greater love has no one than this, that he lay down his life for his friends."

Jesus, John 15:13

"Imitating Christ is opening the door to friendship."

Billy Graham

Outside, the snow falls noiselessly from a cold, slate-colored November sky. You have just stepped inside a bright warm greenhouse. Shaking the snow from your coat, you pull off your hat and gloves. The view is stunning: thousands of poinsettias in brilliant reds and whites fill a space of perhaps 12,000 square feet. From your vantage point, it seems the blaze of holiday color could not be more perfect. Row after row of nearly identical, beautifully lush specimens stretch ahead. The gardener moves toward you along one of the narrow aisles between the tables. His faded blue jeans and dark green work shirt contrast dramatically with the blaze of color around him.

Deftly maneuvering the nozzle of a garden hose with his right hand, he carefully touches individual specimens with his left. He fingers the soil of certain pots, testing the moisture content. Occasionally, he bends down to examine a specific plant, inspecting the underside of the leaves with an expert, gentle touch.

"It must make you proud to know you've grown all these beautiful plants," you remark. "They're so perfect!"

The grower looks up with a knowing smile. "I wish that

were true." He flips the control on the nozzle and the water sputters to a halt. Gesturing to the plants around him, he says, "They might look that way from a distance, but up close it's a different story. Some in this section, for instance, are showing fungal leaf spots. I'm not getting the right air circulation from that furnace up there, and it has created a little pocket of damp air—kind of a microenvironment. Over there," he waves the nozzle toward a section of pink poinsettias, "I tried a new variety, but it's been slower in forming bracts than the kind I'm used to. I'll have to figure a way to schedule them differently next year." He frowns in concern as he gazes over the sea of red around him.

"Well," you smile and shake your head, "they still look great to me."

Behind the facade

It is tempting to see the people with whom we come in contact like we see the lush flowers on a visit to the greenhouse. Our culture has taught us to look good. We dress for success. We are conditioned to say, "I'm fine!" "I couldn't be better!" "Life is good!" These are the automatic responses we give and receive at work, in our neighborhood and even among our friends and family. It's easy to miss reality. We tend to gaze across the ocean of faces and see only a "perfect crop": men and women looking their best.

At first glance, we scan the surface and conclude "all's well." It is less troubling to ignore weeds of anxiety, loneliness and hurt that have been growing in the heart of an acquaintance. It is simpler to overlook the hollow pain of a soul starved for relationship.

Behind their pleasant facades, the deep longing for meaningful friendship is a reality for countless people. A sense of isolation is one of the most disturbing trends of our modern world. Men and women are driven and intense, pursuing careers and dreams with an air of success, disguising their lonely, anemic souls.

On a recent flight, I had a casual conversation with the young woman sitting beside me. She told me that she had recently been transferred from the West Coast where she had lived all her life to a large East Coast city. She had a great job that she said, "I absolutely love." This young lady looked the part. She was dressed for success, confident, engaging and assertive, with a cell phone in one hand and a laptop in the other.

Our conversation continued easily until I asked a question that touched a hidden part of her life. "How do you make friends in a new city?" Her confidence vanished. As tears filled her eyes, she quietly said,

"I have no friends." As we continued to talk, she shared with me the difficult task of trying to connect with someone to form a meaningful friendship in a new location. This young woman is not an isolated case. She was simply describing one of the most common and desperate needs in our world today.

How do you meet friends in a new city? The bar and party scene that is glamorized in pop-culture typically leads to hurt and disappointment, not fulfilling relationships. We have been told that this freedom brings happiness. But Hollywood producers omit the personal costs of the "free love" party life on the screen.

Jesus calls you "friend"
∞

Jesus shows us how to relate to the people with whom we come in contact. He models for us how to be a true friend. He is much like the greenhouse gardener I mentioned earlier. Through the pages of the New Testament, you can see Jesus moving through a group of people, gripping a hand or clasping a shoulder. He crouches to meet children at their level, hoists a toddler onto his shoulders, and recognizes individual problems and pain. Jesus intentionally involved himself in the everyday concerns of people, interacting with them as friends.

Jesus saw things nobody else would see. He noticed the little tax collector who had climbed up a tree to watch him walk past. The woman with chronic bleeding couldn't remain anonymous in the crushing crowd after Jesus felt her touch his cloak in a desperate bid for healing. Each of the local young men Jesus called to be his apostles did not escape his notice— even out on a boat or sitting behind a tax booth.

Jesus does not ignore your loneliness. He does not excuse your withdrawal from the light. He cares too much to ignore or to make excuses for who we really are. He keeps accepting us "as is." I see the expression of warm concern on his face. In his eyes, there is a twinkle that was born in the depths of a heart full of love. Jesus sees not only who we are, but who we can be.

"I have called you friends," Jesus said to his apostles during their last meal together. "For everything that I learned from my Father I have made known to you" (John 15:15b). Jesus tells us a lot in that statement.

1. The barrier between God and humanity has been broken down. God calls us "friends."
2. Friendship is a process, something that must be learned. Jesus spent three intensive years teaching and mentoring his disciples. Friendship takes loving effort. Discipline. Determination. Design.
3. Friendship is something to be passed on. Jesus "made known" what God had taught him and asked the apostles

to tell others. We are befriended so that we may in turn extend friendship.

Jesus is God, our Friend

Some people see God as being far removed from the world and society. If he is there at all, they believe God is:

- Unapproachable
- Not someone with whom you want to spend time
- Distant
- Restrictive
- Demanding
- Fearsome

The Bible gives us an accurate view of who God *really* is:

- Redemptive
- Just
- Forgiving
- Holy
- Loving
- Accepting

Bethlehem wrote a new chapter in human history. A baby was born there in a borrowed manger. God arrived on our turf.

God's choice to become one of us is a magnificent gesture of friendship. That he would leave the lofty splendor of the heavens to walk the wastelands of the world is beyond comprehension. He left the company of worshiping angels to stroll alongside us, feeling our pain, frustrations, hunger and temptations, underscoring the lengths to which God will go to express his love. In *Making Friends and Making Them Count*, Em Griffin observes,

> Perhaps that's why God took human form. "Each of you should look not only to your own interests, but also to the interests of others. Your attitude should be the same as that of Christ Jesus: Who, being in very nature God, did not consider equality with God something to be grasped, but made himself nothing, taking the very nature of a servant, being made in human likeness. And being found in appearance as a man, he humbled himself and became obedient to death—even death on a cross!" (Philippians 2:5–8). He understood our need for a living model . . . the visible image of the invisible God.

He became our friend to model what he expects of us, to create a pattern for us to follow.

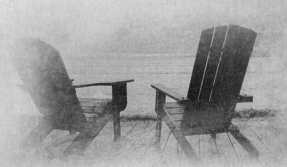

When the paralyzed man was lowered to Jesus through the roof, Jesus told him, "*Friend,* your sins are forgiven . . . get up, take your mat and go home" (Luke 5:20,24, italics mine). Jesus is fully God. He has the power to forgive your sins and heal you. Yet, he calls you, "friend."

Jesus was well liked

Wherever Jesus went, crowds followed him. Three of the Gospels record Jesus' words to "let the little children come to me" (Matthew 19:14; Mark 10:14; Luke 18:16). Children loved to be with him, and Jesus openly welcomed them into his presence. In his book *Man to Man,* Dr. Charles Swindoll calls this kind of approachability "winsomeness." He chides the "stern, somber Christian who has developed the look of an old basset hound through long hours of practice in restraining humor and squelching laughs." Jesus models a life well lived.

Mark tells us that a large crowd "listened to him [Jesus] with delight" (12:37). The Greek word translated as "delight" (rendered "gladly" in the King James Version) means "sweetly, with pleasure." To see Jesus, the King of Kings, only as a conquering soldier, wielding the sword of judgment in a march from heaven against the forces of evil, is to see only one part of his divine personality. Jesus models friendship.

One of my dad's favorite stories was about a little girl who went to stay with her grandparents for a few days. (Thankfully not all grandparents fit this image.) This girl's grandparents lived in the country on a farm. One hot summer day, the little girl's energy was getting on her grandfather's nerves. It seemed to her that everything she did was wrong, and her grandfather scolded her over and over. He finally resorted to scolding, "Christians don't do things like that!"

The little girl went outside and began walking down the country lane that led away from the farmhouse. As she walked, she noticed some little lambs skipping through the field. In her frustration, she said, "Lambs, I know *you* aren't Christians, you're having too much fun!" Farther down the lane, she watched a brown colt prancing through the field. She shook her head and called to the colt, "I know you will never make it to heaven. You are enjoying life too much!"

As she rounded a bend in the lane, the little girl spied an old mule standing under an overgrown apple tree. Occasionally, his tail flicked up to swat a fly. She shook her head and sighed, "Mule, you *must* be a Christian. You are just like my grandfather!"

I hope that story reminds you, as it does me, that we are called to demonstrate the joy of the Lord in our actions.

Bruce Marchiano portrays Jesus in The Visual Bible's pro- duction of *The Gospel According to Matthew*.

Immersing himself in God's Word as he prepared for this role, Marchiano became convinced that his mission was to portray Jesus as a man of joy. In his book, *In the Footsteps of Jesus: One Man's Journey*, Marchiano says he threw himself into his work, representing Jesus as a man totally involved in the lives of the people surrounding him. If his disciples were in a boat preparing to shove off, Marchiano's Jesus wasn't sitting alone in the stern, "solemn and serenely detached" with Hollywood hair motionless in the wind. Marchiano depicted Jesus "pushing and pulling . . . lifting and hoisting, and loving every second of it. He'd be grinning from ear to ear, enjoying the astounding machinery of his own human body and the breathtaking dynamics of his marvelous creation—the sea, the wind, the waves, the sunset."

Jesus sought friends

Jesus modeled friendship in his approach. Most of our friendships seem to "just happen." Two little girls in the same class become best friends because they both like sprinkles on their ice cream cones. College roommates from differing backgrounds are thrown together by the room draw and become close friends because they like the same music. Few friendships are intentional. Have you heard of someone leaving home in the morning with the express purpose of "finding a best friend today"?

Jesus did just that. The Bible says, "he came to his own" (John 1:11). He made himself vulnerable to the whims of his own borrowed generation. He handpicked his first disciples, going to meet them at their job sites and recruiting them. He initiated unlikely contacts, stopping to talk with a tax collector and an outcast Samaritan woman. Jesus wasn't afraid of the criticisms of others. He had a higher purpose. He didn't excuse wrong behavior; he made people desire to change when they witnessed his life first-hand. Jesus intentionally sought out people to befriend.

Jesus accepts the rejected

Jesus modeled friendship by openly pursuing people nobody else cared about. He moved freely among the socially unacceptable: lepers, cheating tax collectors and prostitutes. He met people *where* they were and *as* they were. The Bible says he loved us "even while we were sinners" (Romans 5:8).

"You did not choose me, but I chose you to go and bear fruit —fruit that will last" (John 15:16). This statement wasn't only for the twelve apostles gathered with Jesus that night in Jerusalem sharing the Last Supper. It wasn't only for the men and women who had followed him the previous three years. It was a pattern and a mandate for all of us.

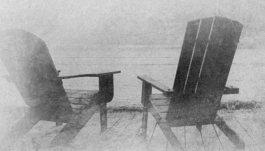

Jesus got down in the trenches of life and held the hands of the trembling. He wiped a fevered brow. He lifted those who had stumbled and fallen. He whispered loving acceptance to those whose ears were filled with the curses of the crowd. He showed us how to be a friend.

It was a friendship without strings. Jesus doesn't love us "if." He just loves us. His love is not based on our merits. He said, "You did not choose me, but I chose you . . ." (John 15:16). There is no agenda other than the one that caused him to lay down his very life for us, to reconcile our relationship with God. As Adrian Rogers writes in *How Knowing Jesus Will Help You be a Friend*, "The foundation of the whole process is Jesus loving me. Because of his acceptance of me, and because of the friendship I have with him, I can become a true friend to others."

Obedience, God's framework for friendship
∞

During the Last Supper, Jesus' final meeting with the apostles before his death, he also said, "You are my friends if you do what I command" (John 15:14). The word *if* prefaces a condition: "You may have a cookie *if* you wash your hands." "You have a better chance at getting a good job *if* you graduate from high school."

We have seen that friendship with Jesus is unconditional. In his words and actions, Jesus repeatedly welcomed people into a personal relationship with himself regardless of age, gender, social place or the most "colorful" history of sin. But what about this verse? Was Jesus putting *conditions* on his friendship by demanding obedience? Does that contradict what Ted Engstrom identifies in *The Fine Art of Friendship* as the primary principle of friendship: "the principle of demanding nothing in return"? Can friendship be unconditional and have conditions at the same time?

Without Jesus, it probably can't. But when faith is factored in, a *supernatural dynamic* is involved. Jesus said, "I am the vine; you are the branches. If a man remains in me and I in him, he will bear much fruit; apart from me you can do nothing" (John 15:5). What's the condition? We must "remain in" Christ. Obedience *is* required, but we cannot obey Jesus by our own strength or determination. Apart from Jesus, we can "do nothing." This is where the *supernatural dynamic* comes into play. God's non-exclusive, all-knowing, ever-present, all-encompassing love for us through our faith in the Lord Jesus becomes both our Source *and* our Supply, supernaturally. He is the Source of our friendship with God and the Supply for all conditions.

God's purpose is a loving purpose. His design is redemptive, not destructive. His plan is for our highest good, even in the face of our deepest rebellion. His love has no limit. His mercy has no bound- ary. His forgiveness

has no exceptions. He can love us at our very worst with the very best of intentions. That inclusive *design* for friendship with God existed before the first planets spun in orbit. "He chose us in him before the creation of the world . . ." (Ephesians 1:4–8).

In the same conversation with his apostles where Jesus laid out his "condition" for friendship, he also said: "If you obey my commands, you will remain in my love, just as I have obeyed my Father's commands and remain in his love" (John 15:10). The unbridled, free-flowing dynamic of God's unconditional love and acceptance is contained within the framework of obedience to his commands. Jesus modeled that in his life on earth, and we are called to follow his example.

The framework is built upon God's nature. The core truth of that framework is that God cannot act in a way that contradicts his nature. God is love. He expresses that love in a barrier-free relationship with us. Consequently, he expects our relationships to reflect that same love. To "remain in his love," we must align our will to his. "You are my friends if you do what I command" (John 15:14).

Jesus' sacrificial purpose

Nowhere is the sacrificial aspect of friendship more clearly revealed than in the life and purpose of Jesus. Jesus told his disciples, "Greater love has no man than this, that he lay down his life for his friends" (John 15:13). That was more than a sermon for Jesus. It was a way of life.

The biography of our Lord is filled with incidents when he sacrificed his own comfort for the sake of someone else. On many occasions, in spite of a grueling preaching and teaching schedule, Jesus committed himself to taking detours: to a tax collector's house, to a well in the town of Samaria, and to the countless people he stopped to heal, teach and bless.

No one was exempt from his friendship. He even wept over the broken relationship with his enemies. One of the most stirring scenes in Scripture is Jesus standing on a hill overlooking the city of Jerusalem. In its synagogues, religious zealots who misunderstood his cause were seeking every device to oust him from influence. In spite of their hatred, Jesus' heart was broken over their rejection of his friendship. He wept (Luke 19:41).

At the cross, biblical friendship is epitomized. The journey to that horrific, yet wonderful scene is posted with the signs of God wanting a relationship with individual people. Face-to-face with Moses, God first handed down his Word on cold slabs of stone to seal his covenant with humanity. But the Ten Commandments were more than rules and regulations. They were God's overture of friendship—outlining a way to live in relationship with a Holy God. The disease, division

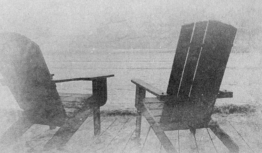

and death that broke the hearts of God's people in their wanderings broke the heart of God. So he gave them a law. He promised them blessing and health for living within the safety of that law.

Still, people broke the law. They turned their backs on blessing and safety. They turned from a relationship with the Almighty to go their weak ways. That, too, broke God's heart. So he offered the greatest solution: salvation. And he made the greatest sacrifice: his only Son.

Born in Bethlehem in the damp cold of a cave stable, Jesus was sent from heaven to express God's unconditional love. Living with us on the dusty streets of time, Jesus modeled reverence and obedience to his Heavenly Father. That obedience resulted in his death. Refusing to abandon his Father or his commitment to each of us, Jesus offered his own life as a price for our broken relationship with God. It was the ultimate act of friendship.

Every terrifying scene, from the travesty of the courts to the agonizing crucifixion on Golgotha's hill, was a dramatic revelation of mercy and grace. God so desired a relationship with us that he was willing to turn his back on his only Son, Jesus. Jesus died alone and lonely. Separated from God's holiness because of our sin, Jesus cried out from the cross, "My God, my God, why have you forsaken me?" (Mark 15:34). He experienced the very worst so that he could offer us the very best.

In his death, Jesus demonstrated the length to which he would go to prove his friendship with us. In his resurrection, he displayed the power over death and the hope of eternal life offered to us through reconciliation with God.

Jesus' purpose for friendship

Jesus' purpose for friendship lies in his loving acceptance of others: friendship is to be passed on. Jesus taught us by his life example that all of our experiences, painful or pleasant, are for the express purpose of glorifying God (John 12:27–28). How do we glorify God? By loving God and by serving others.

Jesus said, "'Love the Lord your God with all your heart and with all your soul and with all your mind.' This is the first and greatest commandment. And the second is like it. 'Love your neighbor as yourself . . .'" (Matthew 22:37–39). Loving God is lived out in daily life by loving others. You are called by God to love the people around you.

Jesus' life was one of reaching out, touching, healing and teaching others to do the same through the power of his name. Jesus endured the wrath of Roman soldiers, encouraging his followers to help the soldiers bear their armor (Matthew 27:30; 5:41). Jesus' back was whipped and mutilated, but he asked his disciples to be patient and compassionate in their suffering (John 19:1; Matthew 5:39).

No one lived among people like Jesus.

His friendship was to be imitated and then passed on.

The astounding truth is this: he expects us to be just like him, not by some tyrannical rule and authority, but by an open invitation. An invitation to:

- Drink from the well of his supply.
- Make him the resource for living among the lost and lonely masses.
- Take up his cross of commitment and carry it through the streets of life, as a living witness of mercy.

Jesus doesn't expect us to be pioneers. He does not ask us to sail uncharted waters. He gives us an example to follow. He has pioneered a friendship that loves through adversity. Jesus has taught us how to be friends.

> *"My best friend is the one who brings out the best in me."*
>
> HENRY FORD

> *"Friendship is a way God loves us using human beings.
> . . . I see people drawn to you because of the friendship
> that emanates from you and because they can sense
> that you sincerely care about them."*
>
> STEPHEN SMOKER

A Testament to Friendship

"If one falls down, his friend can help him up. But pity the man who falls and has no one to help him up!"

ECCLESIASTES 4:10

"You never know the best about men until you know the worst about them."

G.K. CHESTERTON

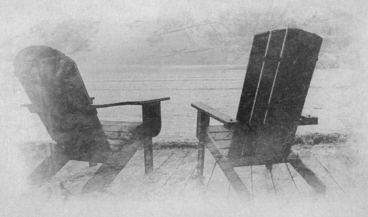

In Earnest Gaines' book *A Lesson before Dying*, principal character Grant Wiggins reluctantly begins interacting with a prisoner named Jefferson. Grant's assignment is to change Jefferson's image of himself from a hog to a man before his scheduled execution.

The two men have little in common. Jefferson is poor and illiterate. Grant is an educated elementary school teacher. For different reasons, both experience alienation and injustice in pre-civil rights era America. As he helps Jefferson realize dignity and self-worth, Grant discovers that his own stony exterior is capable of being pierced.

A few days before he is executed, Jefferson writes in his journal:

. . . an you look so tied sometime mr wigin i just feel like tellin you i like you but i dont kno how to say this cause i aint never say it to nobody before an nobody aint never say it to me. . . .

There is something desperate and dreadful about the word

"loneliness." Fear of being alone and unloved often reaches back to our childhood years. We may choose solitude for a period of time, but we seldom choose to be lonely.

Can you remember the first time you felt lonely? I can. When I was four years old, I went home with my older sister and her husband to spend the night. I was excited about the adventure and all was going well. Then, in the midst of playing and having fun, I looked out the front door as the sun was setting. Suddenly, my feelings changed. I can still remember the heavy sense of loneliness in the pit of my stomach.

If you are thinking, "that's just a typical case of youthful homesickness," you are right. But it is a picture of the loneliness we can experience even when we're surrounded with people who love us and care for us. Loneliness can strike unexpectedly.

I have experienced that same sharp feeling of isolation as an adult. In 1989, I arrived in Romania three days after the national revolution had culminated in the execution of the brutal communist dictator Nicolae Ceausescu and his wife Elena. It was a difficult and exciting time to be with my brothers and sisters in the Romanian church. At their request, despite the political upheaval, I kept arrangements made months earlier to minister in several "underground" and government-sanctioned churches. During the trip, I was privileged to see God's mighty hand working in Timisoara, the city that sparked the revolution.

In the fragile aftermath of the Romanian revolution, no one knew what was going to happen. The infamous secret police were in hiding, and the fearful talk on the street was that they could burst on the scene at any moment to regain control. The sound of gunfire was a way of life.

Late one evening after dinner in a friend's home, I made my way along the city streets back to the hotel where I hoped to connect with my friend and partner in ministry, Ed Scearce. Earlier that evening I had preached at First Baptist Church. Ed had preached at another church in the city. After the service, I was invited to dinner in a church member's home. From the apartment windows, we watched and heard gunfire only a short distance away as we ate. My hosts did not want me to return to the hotel. They felt it was too dangerous. But I insisted that I must return in hopes that I could reconnect with Ed. I finally arrived back at the hotel, only to find it surrounded by army trucks and armored vehicles. Soldiers searched and questioned me before clearing me to pass through their ranks into the hotel. It was an unnerving experience, to say the least! I was overjoyed to find Ed waiting in our room.

Throughout the night, gunfire and the movement of army personnel and equipment continued. It appeared as though the revolution battle was breaking out again. I remember thinking and feeling many things that night.

Should we stay in Romania? Should we try to make it to the Hungarian border? Will I live through this? Will I ever see my wife, Barbara, and our children, Michelle and David, again? The feeling I remember most is the heavy sense of loneliness. I thought, *it is one thing to be lonely at home, but to be lonely in a distant country is definitely not fun!*

In the midst of all the isolation and uncertainty of that night, God gave me peace and comfort as I turned to him in desperate need. His Word's promise became a reality in my life: "Have I not commanded you? Be strong and courageous. Do not be terrified; do not be discouraged, for the Lord your God will be with you wherever you go" (Joshua 1:9). His presence, peace and comfort allowed me to rest secure in his care, and I went to sleep.

Of course, my family will be quick to say, "What's the big deal? You can sleep *anywhere* through *anything*!" But that is one night that physical exhaustion would not have brought sleep without the Lord's assurance of protection. Not only did the Lord give me comfort that night, I had the comradery and encouragement of a close friend. Ed, thanks for your friendship. I don't know how I would have made it without you. That is a night I will never forget.

Biblical friendships

The Bible is not silent when it comes to the important issues of our lives. It speaks clearly and personally. As the psalmist writes, the Word of God is a "lamp to my feet and a light for my path" (Psalm 119:105). Not surprisingly, the Scriptures guide us in cultivating our relationships with others. The Bible itself is a document of friendship. It is a testament—an agreement, a covenant between humans and our Creator. It is a message of communication, reconciliation and promise. The Bible is God's personal message to us.

As a heavenly antidote to the trauma of isolation and loneliness, God's Word introduces us to the treasures of friendship. We've found that God is a relational God—the Creator and Source of friendship. Jesus' life, as seen across the pages of the New Testament, is the perfect and ultimate model of friendship with God and with people. The Bible, God's Word, is a gold mine of practical wisdom on friendship.

The Bible details the treasures and traumas of friendship in the lives of biblical characters. Moses, Abraham, King David and Jesus demonstrate vital friendships with God and with the people around them. Their friendships and many others are narrated across the pages of Scripture. In dusty wilderness camps, on bloody battlefields and along the shorelines of Galilee, friendships frame the trials, daily events and life-changing ministries of the Bible.

Loneliness is a chronic problem in modern society, but

it is not a by-product of the computer age alone. It is a stifling cloud that has blocked the sunshine of life for scores of individuals throughout the centuries. The Bible describes its awful impact. Many godly men and women throughout Scripture experienced times of intense loneliness. The Sons of Korah, a temple choir during the reign of King David, sang a psalm of lament that graphically expresses feelings of abandonment and distance from God. "You have taken from me my closest friends and have made me repulsive to them. . . . You have taken my companions and loved ones from me; the darkness is my closest friend" (Psalm 88:8,18).

It might seem strange to sing such mournful songs in church, but God wants us to honestly express our feelings to him. He is not intimidated by our frustrations. This is exemplified countless times in the Bible. On the heels of a great victory, the brave and mighty prophet Elijah was suddenly running for his life. From his hiding place in a cave, the overwhelmed prophet complained to God, "The Israelites have . . . put your prophets to death with the sword. I am the only one left, and now they are trying to kill me too" (1 Kings 19:10).

God as "Friend"
∞

Why does God's Word detail so many human friendships along with their sorrows and failings? It is part of God's involvement in individual human lives. It's an expression of his desire for relationship with us. The most common word for "friend" in the Old Testament is the Hebrew word, "rea`." It has at its root the idea of association, whether a casual acquaintance or an intimate relationship. One of the most outstanding friendships in the Bible is between God and Moses, the man chosen to lead the Israelites out of slavery in Egypt. The Bible tells us, "the Lord would speak to Moses face to face, as a man speaks with his friend" (Exodus 33:11).

A different word for "friend" is used to describe God's relationship with the patriarch Abraham. "'Ahab" is the Hebrew word identifying deep affection or loving companionship (2 Chronicles 20:7; Isaiah 41:8). It is used more than 200 times in the Old Testament. This is the kind of affection that characterized the friendship between David and Jonathan (1 Samuel 18:1). Such a friendship is a blessing!

In the New Testament, the most commonly used Greek word for friend, "philos," covers a spectrum of association from casual to intimate. Philos is primarily associated with friendship love. By reading each account in context, we see Jesus operating within concentric circles of relationship, calling each group "friends." At the outermost ring are the "crowds," the world in general. Within the next ring are the disciples, the followers of Jesus. Closer still, are the

twelve apostles, personally chosen by Jesus to learn his message and equipped to spread his gospel. Closest of all are Peter, James and John, Christ's "inner circle." His conversations with these three apostles are often recorded in the gospels. Only Peter, James and John were with Jesus when he was transfigured, revealing his glory as God's Son (Matthew 17:1). Some scholars speculate that Jesus even had a best friend, John, "the disciple Jesus loved" (John 19:26).

"As thine own soul"

Em Griffin recounts an Arabian proverb. A true friend is "one to whom one may pour out all the contents of one's heart, chaff and grain together, knowing that the gentlest of hands will take and sift it, keep what is worth keeping and with the breath of kindness blow the rest away." The Bible describes such close, intimate friendships.

There is an easy grace and comfort in a close friendship, all the more special because it is reserved for so few. Henry Adams said, "One friend in a lifetime is much; two are many; three are hardly possible." Some people share an uncommon bond. As God's Word reminds us, "A man of many companions may come to ruin, but there is a friend who sticks closer than a brother" (Proverbs 18:24). The King James Version describes a specific kind of close friend as one who "is as thine own soul" (Deuteronomy 13:6). The Old Testament prince, Jonathan, experienced this bonding with the shepherd David: "And Jonathan loved him as his own soul" (1 Samuel 18:1, KJV).

Pain in friendships

∞

Investing ourselves in friendship also opens us to pain, including the searing pain of betrayal. In the midst of Job's anguish, his three friends heaped blame and criticism on him. Job cried out, "A despairing man should have the devotion of his friends" (Job 6:14). The psalmist King David mourned, "Even my close friend, whom I trusted, he who shared my bread, has lifted up his heel against me" (Psalm 41:9). Jesus must have felt the same anguish when he dipped bread in the dish and handed it to Judas, the "friend" who proved to be a traitor (John 13:26).

The Bible warns us about false friends. It tells us to be alert to those who flock around the rich or who secretly cause dissension (Proverbs 14:20; 16:28). Poorly chosen friendships have an impact on our own souls. Friendship with "the world" is hatred toward God (James 4:4). But despite our best efforts at discernment, investing in a human relationship leaves us vulnerable. Even David, the "man after [God's] own heart," was betrayed by a close and trusted friend (1 Samuel 13:14; Psalm 55:12–14).

Friendship also

opens us to another kind of pain. When we pour ourselves into someone's life, we develop a heart tie with that person. When a friend walks through pain and struggle, we feel it too.

When I met John nine years ago, he was one of the most fit and healthy 55-year-olds I knew. He was eight years my senior, but he could out bench-press me any day. It was decades since he had served as an Army officer, but he still had an unmistakable military bearing and a gracious Southern manner. I had little idea during our first few social contacts that John would grow to be my close friend and a valued partner in ministry. Neither could I have imagined that eight years later I would walk with him through his battle with cancer and finally, his death.

I am still growing to understand the impact that John's illness and loss had on me. The last year of our friendship was painful in many ways. It was a year of ups and downs, encouraging signs and disappointments, frustration and the struggle to understand what my friend was feeling. It was something I would never want to relive. Yet, I am also reminded that John and I had some of our best conversations during those difficult months. I saw John mature in his faith. We both had opportunities to share the good news about Jesus with his friends and family members like never before.

As the pain of that year heals, I still struggle with his death. John's office was next door to mine, and we never used the intercom. It was always, "Hey, John," or "Steve, you need to see this!" I miss him greatly, but I have felt the Lord's healing power in my own life. Through John's illness and death I was brought to a greater dependence on God's grace and strength in my own life.

Do all friendships turn out as we hope? Certainly not. But God made us to live in relationship with others. His intent is for us to experience deep and meaningful friendship. If you are holding back from close friendships as a form of self-protection, you are missing out. Please understand that God loves you. He is your eternally faithful friend and your protection. God's plan for your friendships makes them worth the risk.

Making the investment

Like anything worth having, friendships are costly. They take time and commitment. Friendship is about giving, more than receiving. I have found that when you invest in meaningful friendship, an important biblical principle will be applied to your life: "Give and you will receive. A large quantity, pressed together, shaken down and running over will be put into your pocket. The standards you use for others will be applied to you" (Luke 6:38, GWT). This biblical principle is applicable to all areas of life, including relationships. In other words, if you want friends you must practice being a friend.

If you commit your desire for

friendship to the Lord, I believe God will bless your efforts with meaningful friendship. Like Jesus' story about the "seeds" of God's Word planted in people's hearts and minds, some of the seeds of friendship you sow may fall on stony ground (Matthew 13:3–9). Other seed may be choked out by weeds or briers. But if you keep sowing faithfully, you will reap a harvest of friendship.

I agree with Dr. Jay Kessler, "One of my goals in life is to have at least twelve friends who will sit through my memorial service and not look at their watches." My relationship with my friends is important to me. In fact, I've ranked three priorities for my life:

1. Faith, my relationship with the Lord Jesus Christ.
2. Family, my relationship with my wife, Barbara, and our family.
3. Friends (quite obviously), my relationship with friends.

I am willing to say "no" to many things to maintain these relationships.

The Bible is God's Word on friendship, inviting us into relationship with himself and explaining his design for fulfilling human friendships. In the honest accounts of biblical characters, in wise proverbs and in the words and example of Jesus, we find godly guidance for our relationships today.

We've skimmed through an array of biblical insights on friendship. I hope that you're growing in your trust and expectations for God's Word. It's the most relevant and practical resource on friendship available to you. As we delve into the specifics of friendship—its purpose, dimensions, acts and challenges—we'll use the Bible as our guidebook.

> *"Friendship is a preview of the unguarded, heartfelt oneness of heaven."*
>
> RON SUSEK

> *"Friendship is an invisible bond between two people born from respect and love that overlooks weaknesses and faults."*
>
> W. THOMAS RICE

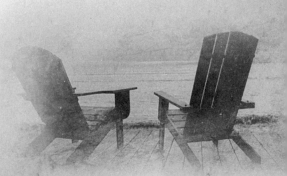

The Dimensions of Friendship

Spiritual, Social and Personal

"Friendship affords us its undivided attentions."

JONATHAN EDWARDS

"But because our expression is imperfect we need friendship to fill up the imperfections. A man of our own type or tastes will understand our meaning before it is expressed; certainly a long time before it is expressed perfectly."

G. K. CHESTERTON

Maybe you've heard of a one-sided friendship. That expression describes the selfish attitudes or actions that may characterize one of the parties in a relationship. It also is an indirect acknowledgement that friendships have various levels or dimensions.

Calvin Miller's classic work, *Singer Trilogy*, is an allegorical interpretation of the New Testament. *The Singer* condenses the gospels. *The Song* dramatizes the first-century Christian church of Acts. *The Finale* focuses on the apocalypse of Revelation. In one of the most poignant passages of *The Song*, the narrator says, "When Earthmaker will not speak to men, they have nothing of importance to say to each other."

In other words, when communication breaks down between God and humanity, it affects the way people relate to each other and how they view themselves. This scenario portrays the three dimensions of friendship. The spiritual, social and personal elements of friendship all must connect and interact to be effective.

"As soon as we are fully conscious we discover loneliness,"

writes C. S. Lewis. Because God created us to be social beings, we cannot truly know ourselves apart from our relationship with him or our relationships with other people. This truth is evident in the life of a great character of the Old Testament. King David was a man of deep and often turbulent emotion. His writings collected in the book of Psalms characterize the many peaks and valleys of David's spiritual and social relationships. Perhaps no other biblical character better typifies the dimensions of inter-personal relationships than David. He was the songwriter of Scripture who, as a shepherd boy, slew a giant enemy soldier with a stone from his sling. David grew up to conquer vast armies by the wisdom and power of Almighty God.

Many of David's psalms reflect his twin fears of being abandoned by God and deserted by friends. That is, failure in the spiritual and the social dimensions of his life. He writes, "[O God,] Do not cast me from your presence or take your Holy Spirit from me" (Psalm 51:11). "I am a stranger to my brothers, an alien to my own mother's sons (Psalm 69:8).

If the spiritual and social dimensions of a person's life collapse, it follows that the personal dimension (self-image, health) will suffer too, as King David portrays in these prayers:

I am forgotten by them as though I were dead;
I have become like broken pottery.

Psalm 31:12

When I kept silent,
my bones wasted away
through my groaning all day long.
For day and night,
your hand was heavy upon me;
my strength was sapped
as in the heat of summer.
Then I acknowledged my sin to you
and did not cover up my iniquity . . .

Psalm 32:3–5a

The spiritual dimension
∞

The first and foremost dimension of friendship is spiritual. We are created as spiritual beings. That innate spirituality affects every area of our lives, including the way we relate to others.

The word "dimension" usually brings to mind something mathematical rather than spiritual. Length, width and height are spatial dimensions. We refer to a "three-dimensional drawing" or "two-dimensional geometry." Paul applied

this mathematical principle to spiritual realities when he wrote, "How wide and long and high and deep is the love of Christ" (Ephesians 3:18). As some Bible commentators have noted, Paul slipped in an extra dimension, depth, to capture the immeasurable fullness of God's love.

Jesus also added a dimension to describe love when an expert in the law asked him, "Of all the commandments, which is the most important?" (Mark 12:28c). In his response, Jesus echoed the *Shema*, the most fundamental teaching of Jewish law.

> "The most important one," answered Jesus, "is this: 'Hear, O Israel, the Lord our God, the Lord is one. Love the Lord your God with all your heart and with all your soul and with all your mind and with all your strength.' The second is this: 'Love your neighbor as yourself.' There is no commandment greater than these."
>
> Mark 12:29–31

Jesus' words vary slightly from the *Shema* of the Old Testament, which says to love God with "all your heart and with all your soul and with all your strength" (Deuteronomy 6:5). Jesus added a fourth dimension: "your mind." In so doing, he emphasized that our love for God should be so complete that it encompasses every aspect of our being.

Jesus added an extra dimension to the second half of the

law as well. When another "expert in the law" asked him, "Who is my neighbor?" Jesus replied with the parable of the Good Samaritan (Luke 10:29–37). The story demonstrates that "neighbor" is any person we may encounter, regardless of social status, race, or religion. The prevailing thought of Jesus' time included only law-abiding Jews as "neighbors." This certainly did *not* include Samaritans (half-Jews) or Gentiles (non-Jews).

I'm afraid that some Christians today hold a similarly narrow view. They put boundaries around their fellowship. Their "No Trespassing" signs may not be displayed outwardly, but they limit their circle of friendships. That is not God's purpose for his people. It does not reflect his unconditional love. In *Let the Redeemed of the Lord Say So!* Eddie Fox and George Morris write, "When the church becomes nearsighted and turns in on itself, it loses its compassion and surrenders its reason for being." The spiritual dimension extends friendship beyond our comfort zone, making every person the "neighbor" whom we are to love like we love ourselves.

The spiritual dimension of friendship is the *God* dimension. As we have discovered, he is the Source of friendship. He put the need for relationship within us. He gave us our emotions and wills. He is the Creator of the

deepest feelings in our sad farewells, joyful welcomes and warm companionship.

Friendship apart from a relationship with Jesus is missing an essential element. He is friendship's life source. When we are out of sorts with God, we are usually out of sorts with the people around us. When the spiritual relationship is short-circuited, it dims the lights on our other relationships.

Take a moment to reflect on this dimension of your life. Are you experiencing the friendship factor of spirituality? In other words, if you are living in an intimate relationship with your Heavenly Father, it will be evident in your interaction with others. God tells us to "love your neighbor," to be a friend. The spiritual dimension of your life has a profound affect on the social dimension of your life.

I'm amazed at God's plan. Only God could design spirituality to work so naturally in the day-to-day realities of our lives. The more time we spend with our perfect holy God, the better equipped we are to spend time with the broken sinful people around us. What an irony! Spending intimate time with God doesn't make us "religious" or place us on some plateau above the masses. Far from it. Instead, when we understand how God sees us, we begin to see his image in the most imperfect people. When we grasp how fully God has forgiven us, we can forgive others freely. When we glimpse the magnitude of his love for us, we can love even the most unlovable out of the fullness of our hearts. That's the power of the spiritual dimension in friendship.

The social dimension

Perhaps you have never stated it like this, but one of your primary purposes in life is to be a friend. When the spiritual dimension of our lives is in place, you and I are enabled to fulfill our main purpose in life: to glorify God in all we do. Our loving Lord works through us to declare his glory to others through friendship.

That's the social dimension in friendship. We are a part of a community. We are not islands unto ourselves. We're connected to all other residents of planet earth. We are neighbors before we are friends.

As we discussed in the last chapter, glorifying God in your friendships does not mean they will be perfect. Can God be glorified in the midst of pain and betrayal? Yes. We may never understand it completely, but when you are seeking God for wisdom and courage in the midst of a broken relationship, he is being glorified. God has a plan for every friendship. Because of God's involvement in your life, you are called to reach out socially. He does not guarantee a 100% find-a-best-friend success rate. But stepping out in obedience to God is something you will never regret.

By answering with

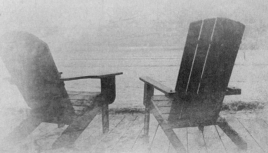

the *Shema*, Jesus seemed to come full circle to his Father's original intent. In the Old Testament, "neighbor" and "friend" come from the same root Hebrew word, "rea`." Even as God's chosen people, the Israelites did not always grasp the full measure of God's unconditional love. Often, neither do we. But God made his intent clear: his people were to love their neighbors, all of them, even foreigners living in their land.

> The LORD your God is God of gods and Lord of lords … He never plays favorites and never takes a bribe. He makes sure orphans and widows receive justice. He loves foreigners and gives them food and clothes. So you should love foreigners, because you were foreigners living in Egypt.
>
> Deuteronomy 10: 17–19, GWT

Again, Jesus adds another dimension to this command. He asks us to love our enemies as well. Jesus' words in Matthew 5:43–45 are paraphrased in *The Message*:

> "You're familiar with the old written law, 'Love your friend,' and its unwritten companion, 'Hate your enemy.' I'm challenging that. I'm telling you to love your enemies. Let them bring out the best in you, not the worst."

We are social beings. Though we may be long past kindergarten, we still look for someone to sit beside, share lunch with and be a friend. We have old high school friends, friends at work and friends who share our hobbies and pastimes. We seek to be friendly and have friends not because it is the popular thing to do, but because it is part of our intrinsic design. Striving to improve our relationships with others is an outgrowth of pursuing our relationship with God. We strive to relate to others because he has willed it. "Let us therefore make every effort to do what leads to peace and to mutual edification" (Romans 14:19). If we seek to do God's will, we work to fulfill his purpose in the social aspects of our lives as in any other dimension.

The personal dimension

Jesus reiterated God's original purpose for friendship by telling us to "love your neighbor *as yourself.*" What does it mean to love "yourself"?

Thousands experience "core shame." As David Thompson describes it in *Holiness for Hurting People*, core shame "spells 'not loved,' stamped in boldface letters across our hearts . . . and hampers efforts right and left to live in love." Psychologists

observe that because so many of us see others through the fractured lenses of our own damaged self-esteems, we cannot enter into authentic relationships.

We project our personal flaws onto others and react defensively to our preconceptions. Men and women consumed with anger assume everyone is hostile to them. Pessimists see the world painted black. Is the physical characteristic you are most self-conscious about the trait you measure in other people? William Barclay notes in *The Daily Study Bible Series*, "The trouble often is that a mind itself nasty will see nastiness everywhere." As Robert Schuller writes in *Practical Christianity*,

> I don't think it's possible for us to love others if we don't have a healthy affection for ourselves. . . . We may even measure God by how we feel about ourselves. . . . We have to be careful not to project our own faulty sense of self-worth upon God and then consequently think that he holds the same low view of us that we hold of ourselves.

Through his parable of the Good Samaritan, Jesus is saying, "The world may be in an awful mess, and people may be flawed. You may not feel good about yourself, especially if you start comparing yourself to those you think are 'better' than you are. But I'm telling you this:

"Love God anyway."

"Love your neighbor anyway."

The Good Samaritan was not bound by the set of rules society had imposed on him. He was not constrained by religious laws. He exhibited self-confidence in the face of a society ruled by prejudice. He did not allow inferiority to stop him from reaching out in compassion. He became a living example of love that is giving, costly and sacrificial. He made a choice; his actions would be governed by a higher power. He would not allow the prevailing social system to force him to live by its corrupt pattern. With no personal gain in view, the Samaritan man did the right thing.

You and I face the same choices in our world. Thank God we're not left to muster up fuzzy emotions and sacrificial acts in our own strength. God is our Source and Supply. The Holy Spirit works in and through you to accept yourself and love the people God places around you. We are free to love our neighbors because we are secure in God's love for ourselves.

Since 1985 my wife, Barbara, has nourished a friendship with Betty, a handicapped woman who had attended our Sunday School class. From the outside, this relationship has all of the signs of a "one-sided friendship." Now in her fifties, Betty never leaves her rural house trailer

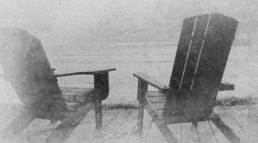

except for trips to the hospital. In fact, she rarely leaves her bed. Her husband is a laborer at a local factory.

Barbara brings "picnic" lunches to eat with Betty in her tiny bedroom. Betty calls Barb frequently, rarely at a convenient time. But Barbara takes time to be Betty's "eyes and ears." She talks about what she's planting in the garden, cooking for dinner or doing at church. In turn, Betty likes to relay a piece of information, usually something she's seen on television—how to grow better tomatoes or an update on a tornado across the country. She also talks about her blessings. She recently told Barb, "If I could give my testimony, I would say so many things about God's goodness in my life."

Betty may not say it like this, but I expect that sacrificial acts of friendship are one of God's brightest blessings in her days spent alone in bed. Taking time to talk with Betty at 7:30 A.M. on a busy day or share a home-cooked picnic meal in her stuffy bedroom can't be done year after year out of a sense of obligation. We are empowered to love selflessly because we are loved.

When Jesus says, "Love your neighbor as yourself" (Mark 12:31), he's talking about a particular kind of love. "Agape" is the Greek word for sacrificial love, love that does not arise from one's natural, instinctive affinity for another. Agape love comes only from God and is fulfilled through obedience to his commands. It is God taking over and doing for us what we cannot possibly do for ourselves. That includes personal acceptance. The Lord Jesus Christ has broken down Satan's demoralizing lies and defeat. Through Jesus we are accepted enough to love everything about us that he loves. Jesus doesn't love our sin. But he loves our self, created in God's image and designed to live with him forever.

The personal dimension of friendship is this: with our confidence and acceptance in Christ, we can open ourselves to ridicule or relationship. We open ourselves to a smile or scorn. We make ourselves vulnerable. Why do we do this? Because it is "agape" love. The love modeled for us by the One who loves us and fulfills us more than any other. Our hearts have the affinity for love because we are first loved. God loves us unconditionally, sacrificially and eternally. That is personal security.

Our purpose then, in friendship, is not self-actualization or affirmation, but as Thompson writes, "reflecting the Living God himself," receiving and repeating "the loving acts of God."

Agape love is the mirror image of God's love for us, reflected in our personal actions toward those around us who have also been created in his image. It is the love through which we realize our Creator's purpose for us: an ever-perpetuating cycle of friendship received and friendship given, all to the glory of the One who is love.

I am sure you have heard the phrase attributed to Ralph Waldo Emerson, "What you are

speaks so loudly I cannot hear what you say." When the spiritual dimension of your life is in balance, your social and personal life will be a bright light for God's glory. People will respond, "What you are speaks so loudly I cannot help but hear what you say."

> *"If you want an accounting of your worth, count your friends."*
>
> MERRY BROWNE

> *"The real need for friendship is most evident when we experience extreme highs and lows in our lives. During the highs, having no friendships is like having a hole-in-one in golf and no one there to witness it and celebrate the moment. Experiencing a tragedy or low point of our lives without true friendship is to experience loneliness at its worst."*
>
> PAUL WEAVER

The Act of Friendship

"Perfume and incense bring joy to the heart, and the pleasantness of one's friend springs from his earnest counsel."

PROVERBS 27:9

"Love must be sincere. Hate what is evil; cling to what is good. Be devoted to one another in brotherly love. Honor one another above yourselves."

ROMANS 12:9–10

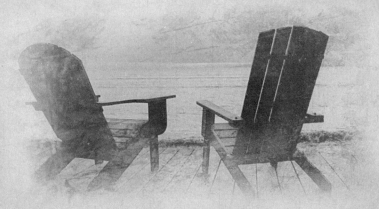

Writing in *Forbes* magazine, Katarzyna Moreno's article "Nuptials" asks, "What does it take to start a business with another person? Chemistry." She reports that Varsha Rao and Mariam Naficy have many things in common, among them a love for writing. Critiquing one another's work frankly, they respect each other's feedback. Because of their similar personalities and interests, they felt comfortable going into business together. They now run a successful Internet cosmetics company. Todd Wagner and Mark Cuban are complete opposites. One is passionate and intense. The other is evenhanded and analytical. Todd and Mark knew each other at the university, but weren't close friends. When they followed different career paths after college, both wanted to "listen to Indiana basketball games wherever they were." This mutual interest led them to form an Internet broadcasting company. Both sets of friends point to "chemistry" as the glue holding their friendships together.

Sometimes the spark igniting a friendship is immediate and intense. That seems to be the case with the Old Testament friends David and Jonathan. After he killed the giant Goliath, David stood before King Saul. When David "had finished talking with Saul, Jonathan [Saul's son] became one in spirit with David, and he loved him as himself" (1 Samuel 18:1).

Other friendships grow with time. The Jewish woman, Naomi, initially could not have been pleased that her two sons chose to marry Moabite women. But over the course of ten years, she bonded with her faithful daughter-in-law, Ruth. Throughout the centuries, Ruth's words have symbolized the loyalty, love and courage of the deepest kind of friendship. "Where you go I will go, and where you stay I will stay. Your people will be my people and your God my God" (Ruth 1:16).

It takes more than circumstances to establish a meaningful friendship. In a *Time* magazine article on "Men Friends," Amy Dickenson records one man's reflection on the "lack of male friends I could talk with about my life." He noted the rarity of friendships "that didn't involve guns, sports or six packs." Most friendships are *about* something: we have aerobics friends, Monday Night Football friends, or office friends. While we enjoy these friendships, we realize that they are essentially one-dimensional, based on a certain set of circumstances. They don't have the depth and durability of a close friendship.

What goes into making a close friendship? Emerson said, "The only way to have a friend is to be one." Add to that Samuel Johnson's advice, "A man should keep his friendships in constant repair." Friendship is an active, ongoing and intentional process, one that requires regular maintenance. Friendships may become comfortable, but they should never become passive, something we take for granted.

Several years ago I realized I was taking a close friendship for granted. The drift was not intentional by either of us. But there was a definite distancing, and I needed to correct my actions because our relationship was too important to be damaged by neglect. When I recognized what was happening, I met with James and told him how I perceived our friendship and what I thought had caused the problem. I asked him for forgiveness.

Let me stress that neither of us had intentionally done anything wrong. We had simply allowed the busyness of work and life to put our friendship on the shelf. I am thankful to say that together we recognized the problem and committed to correcting our actions. We decided our friendship was too valuable to be destroyed by the demands of life. We still have a comfortable friendship, but we are conscientious about maintaining it.

God's Word tells us friendship is a practice, a purposeful investment. Paul wrote, "The entire law is summed up in a single command: 'Love your neighbor as yourself'"(Galatians 5:14). "Love is more than a feeling," writes Rick Warren in *The Purpose Driven*

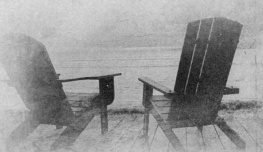

Church. "It is a behavior. It means being genuinely sensitive to someone else's needs and putting them ahead of your own." The highest expression of friendship is the willingness to die for another. Jesus said, "Greater love has no one than this, that he lay down his life for his friends" (John 15:13). This willing sacrifice is dramatized in the friendship of Jonathan and David when the prince risked death at the hands of his own father to defend his friend David before King Saul (1 Samuel 20:30–34).

Laying down one's life for a friend takes on countless forms in day-to-day life. Let's look at several principle acts of friendship outlined in Scripture.

Commitment

To commit to something is to pledge to a particular course of action from initiation to completion. If you start a diet without commitment, chances are you won't make progress, despite your good intentions. Friendship also takes a lot more time and effort than simply having high hopes. A meaningful friendship is not to be taken lightly. Friendships require commitment and devotion, the determination of being "in for the long haul." As a reflection of God's love, true friendship is absolute. Friends are by your side during hard times, as well as the good times. It is not the circumstance, but the substance that determines a committed friendship.

The gospel of John records that when Jesus was crucified,

only four disciples remained at the foot of the cross: three women and the apostle Jesus loved. All of them put their own lives in danger in this reckless act of devotion, remaining with their Friend during his agony and death, committed in their love for him (John 19:25–26).

Commitment to friendships can even extend through generations, according to Proverbs. The writer exhorts us, "Do not forsake your friend and the friend of your father . . ." (27:10a). Without commitment and the trust it builds, other sporadic acts of friendship—sharing, kindness, confidentiality—are hollow, even suspect.

Sharing
∞

Friendship provides a stunning backdrop for the everyday activities of our lives. In both the Old and New Testaments, we see friends sharing their joys, sorrows and possessions. Ruth, the Moabite daughter-in-law, mourned with her mother-in-law, Naomi, after the death of Naomi's husband and sons. Naomi insisted that Ruth return home in hopes of finding another husband and starting her life again. But Ruth wept with Naomi and "clung to her," determined to share Naomi's life despite poverty and widowhood (Ruth 1:14,16).

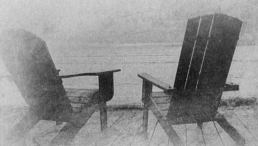

In the parables of the lost sheep, the lost coin and the lost son, Jesus ends each story the same way. The shepherd, the woman and the father each call their friends and neighbors together to "rejoice" or "celebrate" with them over finding what was lost (Luke 15:3–34). People of the Bible act and respond based on their relationships with each other. Paul wrote, "Rejoice with those who rejoice; mourn with those who mourn. Live in harmony with one another . . ." (Romans 12:15–16a).

Being a friend is not always about the big things. It is about being together as part of life and allowing God's presence to flow through you in very natural acts of sharing.

A few weeks ago, I stopped by a friend's house in the afternoon. He and his son were outside in their big back yard, raking the heavy spring grass they had just mowed. My immediate response was, "Dave, you don't need to rake all of that grass! Come down to my house and get my lawn sweeper. You'll have the job done in no time." A few minutes later, Dave drove down the hill to borrow the sweeper. Later that evening he called. "Thanks, Steve. I never realized those things work so well," he said. "I can't believe how much time and energy I saved. I've already ordered one for myself."

Kindness

What must have been going through Moses' mind as he trudged wearily up the mountain to meet God? Not the first time, but the second time. Not carrying the first set of blank stone tablets, but the second set. He had thrown one set to the ground in disgust over the Israelites' spiritual rebellion. Moses already knew that God was angry. He had every right to be angry. But when Moses stood on the top of the mountain, clutching the blank tablets to his chest, God passed by him and announced,

> "The LORD, the LORD, the compassionate and gracious God, slow to anger, abounding in love and faithfulness, maintaining love to thousands, and forgiving wickedness, rebellion and sin. Yet, he does not leave the guilty unpunished. . . ."
>
> Exodus 34:6–7

God wanted Moses to know him for his compassion, grace, patience, love, forgiveness and faithfulness. He placed these ahead of his righteous indignation and anger. God's *nature* required retribution for Israel's sin, but his *friendship* filtered everything through kindness.

The *New Webster's Pocket Dictionary* defines kindness as the quality of being "sympathetic, helpful, friendly, thoughtful, [and] gentle." It's part of God's character and part of the "fruit" his Spirit produces in our lives

(Galatians 5:22). Paul tells us that it is God's "kindness [that] leads you to repentance" (Romans 2:4). Kindness, as demonstrated by our Lord, is an act of friendship.

Encouragement

Encouragement is one of the best gifts you can give a friend. To be affirmed by someone who believes in you is sweet refreshment for the soul. I have had the joy and privilege of being on the receiving end of such encouragement. I pray God will use me in return to speak words of encouragement to my friends.

My friend Dr. Elmer Towns believes in me and in the gift of evangelism God has entrusted to me. Many Sunday mornings at 7:30 we call each other. We talk about our week and where we will be preaching or teaching that day. We conclude our visit by praying for each other over the phone. God has used Dr. Towns in a significant way in my life and ministry. We enjoy working, praying and golfing together. I always feel encouraged when I leave his presence either personally or by phone.

Writing to the fledgling New Testament churches, Paul often exhorted the small bands of believers to encourage each other. They were facing persecutions, false teachers, and the pressures of daily life. Paul told the new Christians in Ephesus to guard their words. "Do not let any unwholesome talk come out of your mouths, but only what is helpful for building others up according to their needs, that it may benefit those who listen" (Ephesians 4:29). He asked the church at Thessalonica to encourage each other with the hope of Christ's return to earth (1 Thessalonians 4:18). To the Colossians, he wrote, "Let the word of Christ dwell in you richly as you teach and admonish one another with all wisdom, and as you sing psalms, hymns and spiritual songs with gratitude in your hearts to God" (Colossians 3:12).

Availability

∞

When a distressed friend rings your doorbell late at night, you don't worry about whether your hair looks like an 80's rock band or that your house is an official disaster area. True friendship is transparent, open and free. With a close friend, writes Engstrom, quoting George Eliot, we feel "the inexpressible comfort of feeling safe . . . having neither to weigh thoughts nor measure words." In his study of *David: A Man of Passion and Destiny*, Chuck Swindoll describes the kind of friend "you can bleed all over" when your heart is broken, one who "won't confront you in your misery or share with you three verses, then tell you to straighten up. . . . An intimate

friend doesn't bail; he's right there with you. You can be your-self, no matter what that self looks like."

"A friend loves at *all* times" (Proverbs 17:17, italics mine). People interfere with our schedules and best-laid plans. But friendship is worth the investment. When a need arises, the act of availability expresses friendship like no other.

Confidentiality

Confidentiality is one of the greatest responsibilities of friend-ship. It is built on trust. Proverbs 17:9 says, "He who covers over an offense promotes love, but whoever repeats the matter sepa-rates close friends." We are also warned, "a gossip betrays a con-fidence; so avoid a man who talks too much" (Proverbs 20:19). In the New Testament, "gossip" and "slander" are listed among heinous sins: God-hating, murder, deceit and sexual immorality (Romans 1:29–30, 1 Corinthians 6:9–10). Marshall writes:

> "If love is the most rugged and most enduring of the ele-ments that go to make up a relationship, then trust is cer-tainly the most fragile. Moreover, once trust is lost it is not easily restored . . . And its restoration always takes time."

Recently while in Sarasota, Florida, I was invited to the city's leadership prayer breakfast. As we fellowshipped together, people shared testimonies of how their lives had been impacted by God through the friendships they had experienced in small groups.

A former member of the U.S. House of Representatives shared an experience that demonstrates the kind of restoration and confidentiality that characterizes God's plan for friendship. While serving as a state representative, he had attended a Christian small group on Capitol Hill made up of Republicans and Democrats. He told us that one day a fellow representative joined their small group. The man broke down in tears and told the others in the group, "Please pray for me! I am living a lie. I have been unfaithful to my wife, and I have a severe drinking problem. I need your help."

This man shared his personal brokenness with congressmen from the opposing political party! If his confession had been leaked, his reputation and career would have been devastated. Yet, he was safe among fellow believers who worked to restore him "gently" (Galatians 6:1). The former representative told those of us gathered in Florida that this man shared his need with the small group over two years ago, and to this day, no one outside the small group knows who he is.

The bond that these men experienced in their small group fellowship is much stronger than a political

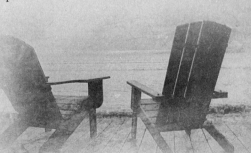

party. They are brothers in Christ, and God is using their friendships to impact their lives for good.

Sacrifice

The act of friendship requires personal sacrifice. First, it requires sacrifice of self: putting another's needs ahead of your own. Every person goes through painful seasons in life when a friend is desperately needed to be a confidante and counselor. That's part of God's purpose for friendship. Willingness to sacrifice my own desire for light-hearted conversation when my friend needs an empathizing ear and serious counsel is part of a God-honoring friendship.

Second, sacrifice means being conscious of the bond that holds your friendship together. The circumstance that sparks your connection may vary, but most meaningful friendships have a bonding that seals the friendship. It may be mutual interests, your personalities "just clicked," or perhaps a shared joy or tragedy brought you together. When we are knit together through life experiences and friendship bonding takes place. We must sacrifice time and energy to maintain those friendships.

Let me add a word of caution. As we discussed in the last chapter, a relationship can become one-sided. Sharing or "problem-solving sessions" may begin to steer in one direction, with one friend increasingly dumping problems on the other.

If a pattern of single-sided "venting" becomes evident, your passive empathizing with a stream of complaints is *not* a loving act of sacrifice. Sharing and confiding in any friendship can engender seeds of gossip and slander, and that is sin. Richard Strauss writes in *Getting Along with Each Other*, "It is impossible to speak of who God is and what he has done, and then go on complaining about circumstances and criticizing people."

How can you distinguish between a friend's legitimate needs and manipulation? Where is the line between sacrificing your personal comfort and getting "taken advantage of"? It's not always an easy call. Most importantly, talk with God about your concerns. He promises to give us wisdom when we ask (James 1:5).

Remember the other acts of friendship. Sacrifice is balanced by kindness and love, sometimes "tough love." Kindness may mean giving your friend a word of honest admonition, not allowing them to sin by gossiping in your presence, or enforcing healthy boundaries out of love for your family and other friends. For me, honesty and kindness have meant helping a friend find a professional Christian counselor. There was a point when I recognized my friend needed professional help. Though I continued to support him and pray for him, I knew that he needed more than I could offer. I

helped him find a good counselor and encouraged him throughout his recovery. In other cases, commitment has meant loving friends too much to allow them to continue unchecked in sin. (We'll talk about that more in the next chapter.) Sacrifice is a purposeful act of friendship, not a "martyr complex."

Touch

"You can impress people from a distance, but you have to get up close to people to love and influence them," writes Rick Warren. "Proximity determines impact." If anyone deserved to stand apart from the crowd, Jesus did. As the Son of God, he could have remained aloof. He could have performed all of his miracles with a wave of his hand or a word from his mouth. But for most of them, he chose touch. Jesus touched unseeing eyes, leprous flesh, shrunken limbs. And he allowed himself to be touched (Matthew 9:21–22).

"From the day we're born, we reach out to hold what we like," observes Griffin. Of the five human senses, four are passive. Sensory data enters our eyes, ears, nose and mouth stimulating our senses of sight, hearing, smell and taste. In this respect, we can say those senses *receive* what is given to them. But touch is different. Touch is active, like friendship. It reaches out to take hold of something. It gives and receives.

As Jesus reached out and touched the individuals in the

crowd around him, was he reminded of his original creative role? At one with the Father and Holy Spirit, Jesus "formed man from the dust of the ground and breathed into his nostrils the breath of life" (Genesis 2:7).

Modeling the personal connection of touch, our Maker also calls us to make touch an act of friendship. In their book, *The Blessing*, Larry Trent and Gary Smalley include "meaningful touch" among their four principles of friendship. In our fast-paced western culture, it is easier to send an e-card than to stop by a friend's office to offer a hug. Every gesture of care is valuable, but don't let them replace "meaningful touch." A hug, a hand on the shoulder, even a handshake can express personal concern that no words can match.

The Bible is rich with wisdom on living out friendship. Reflecting the perfect example of our Maker and Friend, we are given examples and instruction to apply to daily life. It's not abstract theology. The acts of friendship are born out of a living friendship with God. He calls us to reach out in friendship through commitment, sharing, kindness, encouragement, availability, confidentiality, sacrifice, and touch.

"*Always, sir, set a high value on spontaneous kindness. He whose inclination prompts him to cultivate your friendship of his own accord, will love you more than one whom you have been at pains to attach to.*"

SAMUEL JOHNSON

"*Yes, a friend is someone to cry with, someone to help you 'halve' the sorrows of life, but equally important, maybe even more important, a friend is someone to laugh with, someone to help you multiply the joys of life.*"

KERRY WILLIS

Facing the Challenges
of Friendship

"*Better is open rebuke than hidden love. Wounds from a friend can be trusted, but an enemy multiplies kisses.*"

PROVERBS 27:5–6

"*Write down the advice of him who loves you, though you like it not at present.*"

BEN JONSON

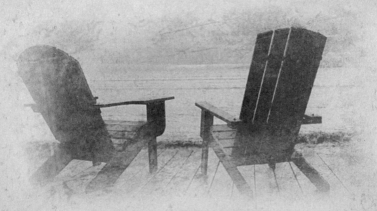

One of today's popular buzzwords is *dynamics*. Developers study population dynamics before selecting a building site. Psychologists refer to the dynamics of interpersonal relationships. Aircraft engineers discuss flight dynamics. Intrinsic to the word *dynamics* are the concepts of flux, motion and change.

Positive and negative dynamics in friendship

The positive side of dynamics is growth. In a friendship, two distinct and often disparate personalities each bring something to the relationship. We have heard the expression that something is "bigger than the both of us." That describes friendship well.

C. S. Lewis said, "Friendship is the instrument by which God reveals to each the beauties of the others." Neil sees abilities in Ryan that Ryan may not have discovered on his own. Elaine finds that Debra brings out a talent that she had been hesitant to share. Ryan feels comfortable telling Neil about an annoying habit he has. "Did you know that you click your tongue when you're nervous?" At first embarrassed, Neil soon realizes that his friend has done him a favor by pointing out something that may have been undermining his credibility at work. When Debra introduces her childhood friend, Jan, to Elaine, Elaine is not jealous that Debra has another close friend. She is delighted to learn new things about Debra. Change and challenges are part of friendship. Dealing with these dynamics positively makes our relationships grow.

Award-winning photographer Howard Bingham has been Muhammed Ali's friend for over 37 years. In the early years of their friendship when Ali was a world-famous boxer called by his given name, Cassius Clay, Howard was an unknown photographer with an incapacitating stutter. It seemed to onlookers then that Howard was the biggest beneficiary of the friendship.

Over the years, their roles have reversed. Howard is now one of the few who can understand Ali's faltering speech. He also works "tough love" principles in urging Ali to keep up his physical therapy and remain functional. Frank DeFord writes of "The Best of Friends" in *Sports Illustrated*. He says, "Now it's Howard moving into the sun, and Ali can't be understood so well, but there is Howard, his great friend, who couldn't speak well, able to speak for him." Muhammed Ali has learned that friendship "cuts both ways . . . Ali needed to be a friend as much as he needed to have one . . ."

The word *dynamics* has a negative side as well. It doesn't take an English degree to see that "dynamite" comes from the same root word. In addition to flux, change and growth, dynamics can involve "dynamite"—disruption, destruction and even violence. We cannot keep everything just like it is now. Life continues to change and relationships are constantly evolving and shifting. Change may result because of a job transition, a move or other life experience. Life is dynamic. This is a fact that we must recognize and accept.

The stretching and changing in friendships can be painful. A relationship is altered by distance and by the seasons of life. Instead of withdrawing, the changes and uncertainty of life should motivate us to work at developing meaningful friendship. Friendship is one of your most enduring possessions.

Value it.

Cherish it.

Invest in it.

Protect it.

You will need your friendships someday. I look forward to sitting in a rocking chair beside an old friend and "remembering when." If that is ever going to happen, I must invest in those friendships today.

Recently, I was at a Thursday morning Bible study led by my friend, Pastor John Sloop. The study

is attended by almost two hundred men of all ages and professions. At the table adjacent to mine, six friends from a local retirement community were sitting together. Pastor John asked us to discuss our favorite phase of life with the others at our tables. It was a great joy to overhear the men at the next table, several of whom were lifelong friends, say, "It can't get much better than this. We have it made! We love spending time with each other, and we have very little responsibility. Life is good!" That kind of friendship doesn't "just happen." Those men had invested in each other. Now they are reaping the dividends.

Morris and Fox quote Maxie Dunham, writing, "The Christian walk is a shared journey. We do not walk alone; others walk with us." Therein lie the difficulty and the opportunity. As we considered in the last chapter, one of a baby's first instincts is to reach out and touch someone or something. Within a few months, another equally powerful instinct becomes apparent. Not only do toddlers refuse to share their toys with other toddlers, they may even snatch away toys and claim them as their own.

In a Christ-centered home, helping a child mature involves directing the child's attention away from self and toward others. That is a dynamic of friendship many adults never quite master. We are naturally self-seeking and self-centered, but healthy relationships require a focus outside ourselves, setting aside our own interests.

The challenges of friendship

∞

Our human nature causes us to gravitate toward the negative dynamics of a relationship, the selfish, dominating, "what's-in-it-for-me," "you-did-me-wrong-therefore-I-will-go-and-do-likewise" dynamics. Even a close friendship faces challenges. We have only to read the story of Paul and Barnabas to see a vivid demonstration of changing dynamics. These early church fathers modeled the worst and the best of friendship principles. There is much to be learned by their association.

1. Disagreement. As an established leader in the early church, Barnabas' name precedes Paul's (originally called "Saul") in their first associations with one another. At first, Barnabas has the role of authority. From the time Barnabas befriends Paul, as recorded in Acts 9:27, through their ministry together in Antioch, their trip to Jerusalem, and in the launching of their extensive missionary journey, Barnabas is the accepted leader (Acts 11:25–30; 12:25; 13:1–3).

The gospel writer, Luke, makes note of "Barnabas and Saul." At one point, he even places "Saul" (Paul) at the *end* of a list of other prophets and teachers (Acts 13:1). However, when Barnabas and Paul leave Cyprus to continue their

missionary journey, Luke writes: "From Paphos, *Paul and his companions* sailed to Perga in Pamphylis . . ." (Acts 13:13, emphasis mine). Barnabas is not even mentioned by name.

From that point on, the dynamics of their relationship seem to change. Empowered by the Holy Spirit, Paul assumes a leadership role, one that thrusts him into the spotlight, while Barnabas seems to fade into the background. In future references, Paul's name most often appears first. There is no record as to why this change took place, but it is evident that Paul takes the lead.

Later, Paul even reprimands the apostle Peter and Barnabas for their hypocrisy in separating themselves from the Gentiles (Galatians 2:11–14). Paul's relationship with Barnabas soon disintegrates into a "sharp disagreement" over Barnabas' relative, John Mark. The rift between Paul and Barnabas was so profound, "they parted company" (Acts 15:39).

Ironically, their disagreement involved the very thing that had initially brought Barnabas and Paul together. Whereas Barnabas had been willing to give Paul the benefit of the doubt when he was a new convert, Paul was not willing to do the same for John Mark. We learn later that Paul's confidence in John Mark was restored (2 Timothy 4:11). We don't know whether Paul's friendship with Barnabas was ever restored to the same level of intimacy. However, Paul later refers to Barnabas with apostolic admiration regarding his work ethic (1 Corinthians 9:6).

We'll never know how God could have used these men if they had followed Paul's later exhortation to the Philippians: "be like-minded, having the same love, be one in spirit and purpose" (Philippians 2:2). But scholars are quick to point out the good that God worked despite Barnabas and Paul's rift. Richard Strauss notes that as a result of the conflict:

- Two missionary teams (Paul and Silas, Barnabas and John Mark) were sent out instead of one, increasing the gospel's impact.
- John Mark's "life was salvaged for God's usefulness." If both men had given up on him, "only God knows what would have happened to Mark."
- This conflict was a growing experience for Paul. Inclined to strong reactions, he later wrote that love "is not easily angered" and "keeps no record of wrongs," lessons he had learned the hard way (1 Corinthians 13:5).

No friendship is insulated from disagreement. When a disagreement threatens your relationship, make a sacrificial effort to come to an understanding. Seek the counsel of a mentor or friend you both trust. Sometimes, you must simply put your friendship ahead of the issue. Enjoy your

friend and let the issue go. Take Paul's counsel: don't be easily angered, keep no record of wrongs, be like-minded and one in spirit and purpose.

2. Busyness. It is easy to fill your day planner or palm pilot with commitments, events and responsibilities, many of which are "good" things. But friendship requires time, undivided attention, and communication. Emerson said, "A friend may well be reckoned the masterpiece of nature." A "masterpiece" isn't generated by a computer program. It's crafted by hand. It requires creative input, personal energy, discipline, adaptability and meticulous attention to detail.

Time is not the precious commodity of the 21st Century only. Ancient Israel's King David wrote, "As for man, his days are like grass, he flourishes like a flower of the field; the wind blows over it and it is gone, and its place remembers it no more" (Psalm 103:15–16). The endlessly "boring" days of a teenager too quickly become the "blink" of an old man's eyes. We can almost hear the urgent poignancy in Paul's words as he faced impending death and pleaded for Timothy to "do your best to get here before winter" (2 Timothy 4:21). He longed for the personal presence of his friend.

Giving our time and personal attention to a friend is often difficult. Everyday distractions and over-commitments threaten to derail even our daily time with God. Communication with God is essential to maintaining a relationship with him. It provides the perspective and balance we need to screen our schedules. How can we expect to know his will, recognize his work or feel his presence if we don't spend time with him? Friendships thrive or flounder in proportion to the amount of communication between friends. Communication is the conduit to honesty and shared vision. It is also the primary tool for troubleshooting and resolving problems.

Busyness is one of the most obvious, yet continually recurring challenges for a friendship. Be aware of it and keep bringing your priorities before the Lord. Every longstanding friendship faces seasons short on spare minutes. You may be facing a period of care giving for small children or aging parents, of unusual job demands or intense education. Look for small ways to communicate with your friends and when possible, to include them in your responsibilities. Ask Jesus to open your eyes to opportunities to connect with friends and to give you peace and security in him above all.

My wife, Barbara, juggled many responsibilities when our children were young. I was often traveling for a week at a time, leaving her in charge of cooking, cleaning, lawn care, hospitality, church and community involvement, car trouble and anything else that came up. In addition, Barb was teaching our two children at home. Still, in the midst of her busyness she made time for her friends. In fact, Barb recalls

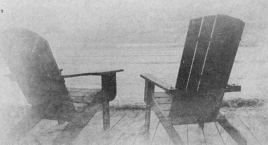

that pursuing friendships was "very important enrichment and encouragement, enabling me to keep going." Though she didn't take friends out for lunch in those days, she made phone calls, taking time to speak meaningful words. Sometimes she invited a friend over for afternoon tea while the children played.

In times of busyness, it may be hard to see the importance of friendship through your overwhelming tasks. But those are the times that you need to invest in relationships. Friends are not another obligation, they are the fuel to keep you going, to bring meaning and value to your life.

3. Betrayal.

> If an enemy were insulting me,
>   I could endure it;
> if a foe were raising himself against me,
>   I could hide from him.
> But it is you, a man like myself,
>   my companion, my close friend,
> with whom I once enjoyed sweet fellowship
>   as we walked with the throng at the house of God.
>   Psalm 55:12–14

Can you feel King David's pain as he writes those words? There is nothing quite as devastating as the betrayal of a friend. I have had friendships that have hurt me deeply. I've had friends who have betrayed the trust that holds friendship together. There may be more, but I immediately think of six relationships that caused significant hurt and disappointment in my life. In each of these friendships, I invested my time and energy into the relationship. Like David experienced, the pain is greater because several of these friends chose to walk away from the Lord, and they no longer felt comfortable being with me. I tried to "rescue" each one, but I regret to say that our friendships no longer exist. In another case, a deep theological difference caused a painful rift in a friendship with a fellow believer. I sought counsel from several Christian leaders to see whether I had a blind spot. Today, we have forgiven each other and my friend is a brother in the Lord, but our friendship is damaged.

I share these experiences not to dredge up the past, but to explain that I have had disappointments and pain in friendship. Still, I believe with all my heart that friendship is worth the risk. If you are still suffering from the wounds of a broken relationship, I encourage you to seek God's healing of past hurt and failure so that you can begin establishing meaningful friendships again.

Betrayal is not something we can control. In those situations, I'm reminded of what a privilege it is to be Jesus' friend. His friendship is unwavering and completely

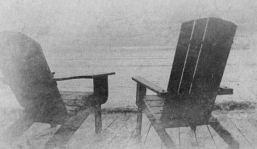

trustworthy. In a world of uncertainties, that's cause for gratitude! We cannot control the actions of our friends. But with
Jesus' model and the strength and wisdom of the Holy Spirit,
we always have the choice of how we will respond.

If you're facing betrayal, dive into God's Word. There's no
"self-help" book that comes close to matching it. You need
God's assurance and direction like never before. The psalms are
a rich source of encouragement and empathy when we're facing emotional pain. Psalm 37 is one of my personal favorites.

It may be tempting to withdraw into a shell and nurse your
wounds, but you must have support. Don't distance yourself
from God's Word or your fellowship with other Christians. Ask
a mature believer for suggestions on a place where you can be
part of fellowship and ministry. If you're not already part of
one, consider joining a small group, a Bible study or a Sunday
School class.

Overcoming the challenges

1. Tough love. In their letters to the early Christians, apostles
Peter and Paul grappled with such problems as encroaching
heresies, backsliding, scriptural misinterpretation and internal
divisions. They skillfully tempered their censure and reprimand
with praise and exhortation, holding believers accountable to
the high standard to which they had been called.

Jesus was the Master of tough love, clearly expressing his

hatred for the sin while affirming his love for the sinner. When Bruce Marchiano first auditioned for the role of Jesus in *The Gospel According to Matthew*, he was given one of the most difficult passages to interpret, the "seven woes" of Matthew 23. In other films, Jesus had been portrayed as a "statuesque figure thundering righteous wrath," as he confronted the teachers of the Law.

> "*You snakes! You brood of vipers!*'—them's fightin' words if ever I've heard any," Marchiano said. But in his quiet devotional time, something kept coming to him: *Desperately love the person you're dealing with.* And that's when he knew that the Holy Spirit was telling him that "Jesus loves people—all people, everybody, no exceptions—even those he was yelling at . . . So though the words were condemning, *the heart would be loving.*"

"Tough love," though never pleasant, is most difficult with close friends. But close friends who are bound together by their mutual commitment to Christ have an advantage. They are wise to "be prepared in season and out of season; correct, rebuke and encourage— with great patience and careful instruction" (2 Timothy 4:2). That takes courage, strength and love. "Do everything in love," Paul exhorts (1 Corinthians 16:14).

Tough love is refusing to withdraw, even when a friend rebuffs you in the midst of her pain. Tough love is continuing to call and invite a friend when his busyness is creating distance in your relationship. Tough love is not obnoxious, but it is persistent. It continues to demonstrate your desire for friendship in meaningful ways. Paul writes that "love is patient, love is kind. It does not envy, it does not boast, it is not proud. It is not rude, it is not self-seeking, it is not easily angered, it keeps no record of wrongs. Love . . . always protects, always trusts, always hopes, always perseveres" (1 Corinthians 13:4–5,7). The "tough" part of tough love is your purposeful decision to keep living out these acts of love, even when you do not feel like it.

When a friend messes up, you must determine that you are not going to give up on him. When others remain silent and avoid her because they don't know what to say, you still make contact. As a friend, you must be honest, and you must simply *be there*. That is tough love—refusing to give up on your friend.

A friend of mine did something he should not have done. His first visit led to another visit, and then another. He was hooked and eventually, he got caught. Because of his wrong actions, my friend experienced shame, hurt, embarrassment and rejection. His relationship with his wife and family was severely damaged, and he lost his job.

But he is my friend, and I refused to abandon him during

this difficult phase of life. After praying about it, I picked up the phone and called him across the many miles that separate our homes. That was a painful phone call. It came at a time of great need in his life. My friend felt abandoned, hurt and all alone. I will long remember the tears shed that day as we talked, cried and prayed together. "I'm calling to tell you that I love you, and I believe in you," I said. "I understand that you've sinned, but I still love you and believe in you." God used that phone call to begin the healing process in my friend's life.

My friend has paid an enormous price for his sin, but our friendship did not need to be a casualty of his wrong actions. True friendship is there for the long haul through life, even during the difficulties. That's tough love.

2. Accountability. For friends who are followers of Christ, tough love is balanced by accountability. Love demands that we not ignore the sins of our friends. Even when the message is difficult, "the pleasantness of one's friend springs from his earnest counsel" (Proverbs 27:9). We must confront as Jesus did, hating the sin but loving the sinner.

Jesus described accountability as an important part of relationships. It seems to be a natural outgrowth of friendship among believers. We both want to please God with our lives and learn to love and enjoy him more

deeply. So as friends, we depend on each other's encouragement and admonition to keep growing and to remain faithful.

As a Christian, don't hold your friends to the same expectations if they don't claim to follow Christ. Understand that these friends are naturally living to please themselves, not God. Demonstrate God's unconditional love and forgiveness for them. I pursued friendship with a guy who didn't know Jesus for years. During that time, he was having multiple affairs, addicted to drugs and more. But we continued to play tennis together weekly. I tried not to be my friend's moral police, but I took every chance to tell him how God desired to have a relationship with him. Decades later, my friend is now living a fulfilled life in a personal relationship with the Lord.

For believers, Jesus gives instructions on the "accountability" part of tough love in Matthew 18. It's a model I've followed.

> "If another believer sins against you, go privately and point out the fault. If the other person listens and confesses it, you have won that person back. But if you are unsuccessful, take one or two others with you and go back again, so that everything you say may be confirmed by two or three witnesses. If that person still refuses to listen, take your case to the church. If the church decides you are right, but the other person won't accept it, treat that person as a pagan or a corrupt tax collector."
>
> Matthew 18:15–20, NLT

I have gone to a friend three times, affirming that I love him and forgive him, but still have to confront his sin. I sought the counsel of church leaders and others, asking, "Do I have a blind spot? What am I missing?" When they told me that I had done everything I could to restore the friendship, I followed Jesus' instructions: "let go."

That's what Jesus is saying when he tells us to "treat that person as a pagan or a corrupt tax collector." Jesus crossed racial and gender barriers to speak with his culture's outcasts. He accepted dinner invitations from tax collectors and let a weeping prostitute wash his feet. But he tells us that when a Christian friend refuses to acknowledge sin, we must finally "let go." We give up the fellowship and intimacy that should exist between friends. That doesn't mean we cross the street when we see that person coming. It simply means that we cannot continue in the close confidence of brothers and sisters in Christ.

The third time I confronted my unrepentant friend, I said, "I love you. I forgive you. But I'm not coming back." That's tough, but it's part of the love and accountability Christ calls us to in our friendships. There are times when you have done all that you can do, and you must release your friendship to the Lord. You cannot force restoration and healing. Place your friendship in God's hands. Your

responsibility before your friend and the Lord is to ensure that your motives are pure. You must be willing to examine your own heart in humility and be accountable to others and to the Lord.

What about "tough love" and determining not to give up on a friend? I believe tough love means we should always live in hope. We may have to release our friendship, but we continue to ask God to bring healing and restoration. You should not live in bondage to a damaged relationship, but take time to pray when the Lord brings that person or situation to your mind.

3. Forgiveness. Since we are flawed human beings, weak by nature and prone to sin, misunderstandings and complications in friendship are inevitable. Even though our just Heavenly Father sees all our flaws, he is "compassionate and gracious … He does not treat us as our sins deserve or repay us according to our iniquities" (Psalm 103:10). However, we are often not so quick to follow his example, especially when we have been wronged by a close friend.

While we may eventually *forgive* a friend, it is even harder to *forget* the wrong. If we hang on to the memory of the wrong, we can never achieve restoration, which is God's intent for forgiveness. He promises, "I will forgive their wickedness and will remember their sins no more" (Jeremiah 31:34b). Too often, we replay the scene over and over in our minds. God's forgiveness is quite different. He hits the "erase" button and wipes the tape clean.

God has modeled forgiveness for us in the most personal and humbling way. He calls us to do the same. In fact, God says that our willingness to forgive people who have wronged us says a lot about our understanding and gratitude for his forgiveness. "Bear with each other and forgive whatever grievances you may have against one another. Forgive as the Lord forgave you" (Colossians 3:13).

Forgiveness is serious business in God's eyes. After explaining what to do "if another believer sins against you," Jesus told a story about a king and his debtors. A servant owed the king millions of dollars he could not pay. So the king ordered that the man, his family and all his possessions be sold to pay the debt. In desperation, the servant fell down before the king, pleading for mercy and promising to repay the millions. The king had pity on him and forgave all his debts.

As soon as he was released, the servant went out and seized a fellow servant who owed him a few dollars. He demanded instant payment and had the man arrested and jailed until the debt could be paid. When word got back to the king, he was furious.

Jesus said, "[The king] called in the man he had forgiven and said, 'You evil servant! I forgave you that tremendous debt because you pleaded with me. Shouldn't

you have mercy on your fellow servant, just as I had mercy on you?' Then the angry king sent the man to prison until he had paid every penny.

"That's what my Heavenly Father will do to you if you refuse to forgive your brothers and sisters in your heart," explained Jesus (Matthew 18:23–35, New Living Translation).

God is merciful to forgive us of massive debts of sin we could never hope to pay. He has modeled forgiveness for us. It is only out of the freedom and forgiveness we have received from God that we can truly forgive others. That's what he calls us to do.

4. Restoration. God's Word explains the principles of restoration. Restoration could be called the active phase of forgiveness. In offering complete forgiveness, we must seek restoration. Of course, even the best intentions cannot single-handedly restore a friendship. But regardless of the result, God calls you and me to step beyond the words of forgiveness to seek true restoration.

Restoration forgiveness works with gentle hands. "Brothers, if someone is caught in a sin, you who are spiritual should restore him gently" (Galatians 6:1).

Restoration forgiveness has a patient, tender heart. "Be kind and compassionate to one another, forgiving each other, just as in Christ God forgave you" (Ephesians 4:32).

Keeping the goals of unity and harmony foremost, *restoration forgiveness* allows the "peace of Christ [to] rule in your hearts, since as members of one body you were called to peace" (Colossians 3:15). "Brabeuo," the Greek word used for "rule" stems from the root word for arbitration or umpire. Friendships take some negotiation, some give and take, but God's Word is the *last word*.

Any time two people are in relationship, there is potential for misunderstanding. When it comes to restoration, it's always "your move." That's right. Friendship calls you to be proactive; to be the first to ask for forgiveness whether you *did* something wrong or it was *perceived* as being wrong. Regardless of the situation, you must be the first to seek restoration.

When trust has been abused and broken, it takes time to rebuild. After you've confronted a friend in tough love and held him accountable, your interactions may feel awkward for a while. That's what takes the commitment to restoration. Don't give up. When friendship is abused, it's costly. Like a jagged tear in a beautiful woven tapestry, the scar may be visible even after it's repaired and stronger than ever. Friendship that endures through the challenges of life is a valued trust. It's worth restoring.

What if you've hurt a friend and you're the one seeking forgiveness? First, take full responsibility. Immediately acknowledge your sin against your friend, and ask for forgiveness. Do whatever you can to make up for the wrong. Resist the urge to withdraw from the friendship because of your embarrassment. Instead, renew your commitment to honoring your friend and investing in your friendship. These are principles I've learned the hard way. Hurting a friend carries its own pain. I pray that I've learned from every one of those mistakes. I'm still learning!

Worth the effort

∞

Gary is a friend of mine who works as a funeral director in Sarasota, Florida. Several years ago, he mentioned to me that it is not unusual to have no one attend a memorial service. Sometimes only a spouse attends. "You're kidding!" I said. Gary assured me that he was serious. He has seen the loneliness, grief and emptiness of a wasted lonely life more times than he cares to recall. I cannot begin to comprehend what it would be like to face the end of life alone.

My mom died at age 89, a testimony to life well lived. Shortly before she died, my oldest brother and I were visiting with her. Floyd asked her who should preach her memorial service. Mom said, "I have five boys who are preachers; if one of you can't do it, we're in trouble!"

After Mom died, the funeral home was packed with family and friends who came to celebrate the memory of her life and home-going. Sorrow and grief were part of the gathering. That's normal. But joy and hope in Christ were evident on the faces of the people who knew and loved her.

I came to this conclusion during those days: the three most important things in life are faith, family and friends. Make no mistake about it. When you look death in the face, and you will, you definitely want those three in place. Yes, meaningful friendship is costly and challenging. It can require major upkeep and painful restoration, but it's worth the cost.

> *"Real friendship is shown in times of trouble; prosperity is full of friends."*
>
> ABRAHAM KUYPER

> *Jesus said, "I no longer call you servants, because a servant does not know his master's business. Instead, I have called you friends, for everything that I learned from my Father I have made known to you" (John 15:15). This is a powerful affirmation from the Lord Jesus of the importance of Christian friendship.*
>
> JOHN GREGORY

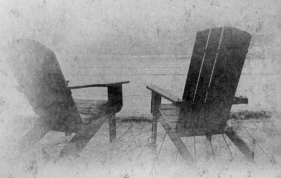

Purposeful Friendship

"Be slow in choosing a friend, slower in changing."

BENJAMIN FRANKLIN

"No man is the whole of himself. His friends are the rest of him."

GEORGE WHITFIELD

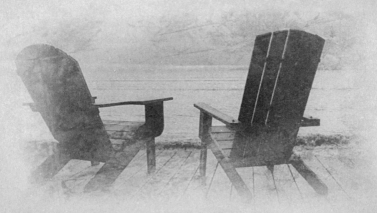

Friendship is one of the most powerful forces in our culture. Its influence touches every strata of society. When its purpose is distorted, the negative effect is far-reaching. Conversely, when its purpose is pure, the positive implications can be life changing.

We've been talking about "purposeful friendships," that is friendships that aren't just a passing whim of the moment or dependent on circumstances and perfection, but friendships that are intentional and deliberate throughout. Purposeful friendships are lived out with resolve, practicing conscious acts of friendship and reconciliation.

In a study to assess the impact of friendship on depression, the Socio-Medical Research Center of London paired eighty-six chronically-depressed women with volunteer "befrienders." Each patient met for at least one hour a week with a specially-trained volunteer. The volunteers mentored the patients by bolstering their self-confidence and encouraging them to make positive changes.

Lisa Peonegro reports the study results in her article

"Friendship Beats the Blues" in *Prevention* magazine. At the end of the study, Peonegro writes that 65% of the women who had been paired with a "befriender" had experienced remission in their depression. The control group reported a 39% remission rate, nearly the same success rate that was to be expected from antidepressant drugs or therapy. Researcher Tirrill Harris concluded, "supportive friendships have the potential to moderate depression for anyone."

The "befriender" program is a good example of purposeful friendship in a secular setting. As in most mentoring relationships, the pairing does not come about spontaneously, but by design (purpose). Each partner enters the relationship with an "agenda," so to speak. A close friendship may develop as the interaction deepens and, in many cases, friendship continues long after mentoring goals are met. Technically, however, intimate friendship is only a by-product of the relationship. At some point it may become the relationship's inspiration, but it is not the spark that initiates the alliance.

Purposeful friendship acknowledges that there is a purpose and plan behind friendship. It was designed by God as a way for us to love him and express his love to others, bringing glory to him. I pray that you're beginning to see purpose and potential in the friendships God has placed in your life.

If you feel lonely despite a full social schedule, don't despair! As we've seen through countless examples, God gave you that craving for strong friendship, an "inner circle" like Christ's friends, Peter, James and John. God invented friendship, and he gave you the desire for a fun, trustworthy friend.

Let's take at step back and look at some basics of purposeful friendship. How can we turn our desire for meaningful friendship into the real thing? How do you start "from scratch"? And how can you befriend an "unlovable" person?

Starting from scratch

Do you recall the successful young businesswoman I met on a flight? Balancing her laptop and cell phone, she had that sharp look of success. She had recently been transferred far from home to take a job she loves in a large East Coast city. But her air of confidence crumbled when I asked, "How do you make friends in a new city?" Tearfully, she admitted, "I have no friends." She began to share with me the difficult task of trying to connect with someone to form a meaningful friendship in a new location.

How do you start a friendship from "scratch"?

Reach out. Remember the proverb, "if you want to have a friend, you've got to be a friend." Be observant. When I'm making a new acquaintance, I like to ask the person questions about his work, family and/or

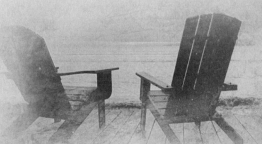

other interests. I ask, "Where are you originally from?" "What are your pastimes?" Notice what he or she is wearing or reading, and ask questions accordingly.

Take lessons. Learning something new with other novices interested in the same pursuit is a great way to connect with people. Since college, my daughter, Michelle, has made several major moves. Almost every time, she has taken some type of lessons. Watercolors, swing dancing, clogging, aerobics … she's learned lots of new things and met many new friends.

When Michelle married and moved to Oahu, Hawaii, her husband was in the midst of residency. Howard spent over 80 hours each week at the hospital, leaving Michelle with a lot of time to fill. One of her best memories of Hawaii grew out of a last minute decision to sign up for outrigger canoe paddling, "Novice B." Little did she know that the canoe club she joined across the street had a history of state championships and a few world-record holding paddlers.

From April through May, Michelle learned the intricacies of ocean canoe paddling with 25 other women of all ages and backgrounds. They paddled, swam, ran and worked out together at least three evenings each week. Their tall Hawaiian coach was demanding. The physical training was rigorous, making her memories of high school track team workouts pale in comparison. Race day competitions, called "regattas," were intense. But by August, Michelle found herself as "stroker" on the race crew of six at the Hawaii state championship, setting the pace for the boat from seat one. More importantly, by the end of the season she had 25 fun supportive teammates, including several valued friends.

Learning something together or pursuing a goal as a team builds a special kind of cohesion. It's a great way to build friendships, whether you are the new kid on the block or you want to expand your circle and meet people from differing backgrounds. Look for something you've been interested in learning, and sign up.

Church—that is, God's people, not a building—is a great place to meet new friends who have shared values and who will encourage you in your relationship with Jesus. Look for a church committed to God's Word, the Bible, and with a wide spectrum of age groups, including your own. Ask about opportunities to get involved and connect with smaller groups within the church—a Sunday School class, a small group meeting in your community, a group centered around one of your interests. Most churches offer many opportunities to connect with others.

Volunteer to do something that you enjoy in your community. Helping other people is a privilege that often leaves the "helper" feeling most encouraged. You may also meet people with similar interests.

For the past twenty years, one of our Wingfield family Christmas traditions has been ringing the bell for a Salvation Army kettle. It has been a rewarding experience, and I have met friends I otherwise would never have known. Though it's usually cold and occasionally snowy, I always anticipate ringing the bell. The smiles and surprising conversations more than compensate for the cold weather.

I knew who Bob was before I started volunteering for bell ringing, but our shared experience brought us together. Bob has watched our children grow up, from the days when all four of us would show up for bell ringing. Occasionally during the past several years, my son, David, helped ring the bell when he was at home during college vacation.

One year when I had to leave early, David completed our shift. Bob showed up, and he and David talked for quite some time. Now, almost every time I see Bob he asks about David. A friendship was born through a common interest and a shared experience of volunteering.

Be a friend. Look for ways to befriend someone else who needs a friend. It is easy to get self-absorbed in loneliness and miss opportunities to connect with people who need a friend just as desperately as you. Next time you're feeling alone or awkward, look for someone else to encourage or set at ease. And keep it up. When the day comes that you're the relaxed "local" or the long-time member, keep watching for a new face who needs a welcome and a friend.

Making "purposeful friends"
out of "casual acquaintances"

∞

One of my closest friendships was born out of a common circumstance. Frank and I both had sons on the Junior Varsity soccer team. Since I was often traveling, I made it a priority to go to all of my son's games when I was in town. Whether they were home or away, I didn't miss David's soccer games. I love a good competition!

Frank was an ER physician, with a similarly challenging schedule. When he was off work, he also went to all of the JV games to support his son, Dan. Frank and I started riding together to the out-of-town games.

Other than both having sons on the JV soccer team, Frank and I had little in common. On our first trip together, he told me that he was raised as an atheist. My dad was a minister who modeled a very personal relationship with Christ. Frank grew up in Denmark. I was raised in southern Virginia. Frank played water polo on the Danish national team. I played high school football.

Today our sons have graduated from college, and Frank is one of my closest friends. It has been exciting to see God's work in his life. As we built our friendship driving to and from soccer games, I worked to keep our conversation purposeful. Our families began getting together for meals and outings. Within a few years, Frank and his wife, Nancy, joined the small group that met in our home for Bible study and prayer. Frank and I also met on Tuesday mornings for accountability with a small group of men. A few years ago, he gave his life to Christ. When I look back on the past ten years, I see that God has worked a miracle in my life and in Frank's life. Our casual acquaintance has grown into a deep friendship.

If you have not moved recently, chances are you have "friends," that is people with whom to socialize. You may have friends to eat lunch with at work, friends to sit beside at your daughter's softball games or friends to chat with at church. These people could be called "casual acquaintances." You have never shared a personal struggle or prayed together. Yet, you have some common interests and feel comfortable with each other. These acquaintances could become purposeful friendships. How?

Going deeper. We become mutual friends with people who share our interests in some way. There has to be that connection, a "gut feeling," to become close friends. Do you have fun together? Do you feel comfortable together? If you cannot connect casually, you cannot go deeper. The sad thing is that many people who *do* connect casually, never take their friendships deeper. There are several keys to opening the door to significant friendships.

Pray. Speak with the Lord honestly about your desire for a close friend. Ask him to bring someone into your path and to open your eyes to recognize the opportunity. When my daughter moved alone to a new town after college, she remembers praying for every little contact she made. She prayed walking up the sidewalk to a Christian coffeehouse, "Lord, please help me find somebody to talk to when I first walk in the door!" She prayed on her way to visit a church by herself. She prayed before she called a new friend she had met. If your desperation for a friend keeps you talking with Jesus, that's great! I hope it becomes a natural part of purposeful friendship for you.

Carefully choose your activities. Can you find a common interest that is conducive to meaningful conversation? For example, you will have more opportunities for conversation if you go out to eat rather than to the movies. Invite a few friends over to barbecue when there's no football game underway. Take opportunities to carpool together, rather than showing up at an event separately. I have personally had some of the most amazing conversations on the golf course, whether or not my game was going well. Whatever you choose to do, keep asking: "Is our time together focused on each other or on the activity?"

Ask questions. It sounds simple, but it is not a skill with which most of us are born. Sure, anyone

can ask those breezy social questions: *How was work? How are the kids? How 'bout them Redskins?* But take it another step or two, and you will see what I mean. Asking a good question takes creativity and true interest. Among men, it's often easier to swap stories than to ask questions. But if you want to go deeper, ask a question. Your story can wait.

In a society where most of us are vying for the spotlight, it is refreshing to have a friend who expresses real interest in our daily lives and thoughts. If it's tough to think of a question on the spot, note questions throughout the day that you would like to ask your friend. You may read something or hear a news clip that sparks an idea. Don't feel odd pulling out your notes when you see your friend. It is flattering to know that someone has been thinking of you and values your input. As your friendship deepens, stay intentional. Keep asking questions, even the hard ones.

Pray together. There is something about seeking God together that adds a whole new dimension to friendship. Instead of dumping problems on each other, you are bringing them together before the One who can carry them away. There is power in agreeing together in prayer. "Where two or three come together in my name, there am I with them" (Matthew 18:20).

How do you begin? Next time your friend shares a concern and you reply, "I'll be praying for you," seize the opportunity! Add, "In fact, can we take a moment to pray right now?" Whether you are on the phone, eating dinner or between games, you are opening the door to prayer. It's okay to start simple. You may be surprised at how much it means to your friend.

Study the Bible together. Much like prayer, this can also be a great way to bring purpose to a friendship. Your local Christian bookstore has many Bible study resources on various topics and Scriptures, including friendship. Choose one together. Studying the Bible is a good way to stay accountable, get a new perspective, and to take your interaction beyond the usual social circles.

Realistic expectations. Approach your friendships with realistic expectations. Just as you are imperfect, none of your friends can perfectly fulfill ALL of your friendship needs and desires. As I think about some of my dearest lifetime friends, I am reminded of the uniqueness each of their friendships have brought to my life. I believe that by God's grace, each one has filled a special "niche."

Karl's has been a strong, "stick-to-itive" friendship that we're both better for experiencing. God has reminded us to pray for each other in some amazing ways during times of crisis. Dave has been an invaluable source of accountability for years. He's faithful and persistent to check in with me, wherever I may be traveling. Ben's example and strength of character

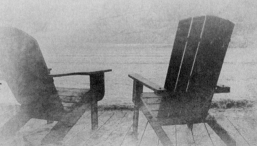

have helped me be a better person. Sam was my best friend in high school. When we reconnected several years ago, we found deep roots with some common experiences from recent years. Sam and I always have a sweet time of fellowship and encouragement. Those are four very different men, and four friendships I cherish in very different ways. Don't burden one friend with a lifetime of expectations. God is faithful to supply your needs.

Sometimes we want to glamorize the process of making friends, picturing some perfect thrilling Hollywood saga. In reality, some of the best friends come in unexpected packages. That's why it's so important to have God's power for discernment and the vision to see his image in the people around us. Making a friend is never boring, but you may have to take some nitty-gritty steps to get out and meet someone.

Befriending the unlovable

Malcolm Muggeridge pointed to the pathos of the human condition in *Something Beautiful for God*. "The biggest disease today is not leprosy or tuberculosis, but rather the feeling of being unwanted, uncared for and deserted by everybody."

It is difficult to reach out to those with whom we feel no natural affinity. Our flesh often recoils at the sight of deep pain and need. But purposeful friendship looks for the image of God in every human being. It affirms the intrinsic value of every person, "the real you, the glorious you" (Colossians 3:4, *The Message*). Friendship with a purpose enables us to see not only who a person *is*, but who he or she *can be* in Christ.

I saw a remarkable transformation in the life of a young man who attended the church where I served as pastor. Chris was 17 years old. He was painfully shy, physically awkward and socially inept. I thank God that several people in our church reached out to him with genuine purposeful friendship. Change did not happen overnight. During his time at our church, Chris never became a dynamic leader. He was not able to reciprocate the investment that others poured into his life. Yet, his youth leader and others persisted in seeing his intrinsic value—who he *could be* in Christ.

Several years later, I had the privilege of completing my graduate work at the seminary Chris came to attend. In many ways, he was still the same Chris. He was a bit awkward and not always socially conscious. But I was continually amazed and encouraged to see the changes in his life. The Lord had transformed him into a bold and confident servant and witness. It seemed as though he would talk to anyone about Jesus! I believe that God used the unconditional friendship lavished on him as a teenager to help transform him into an able man of God.

God designed

friendship to be shared. As God's children, we reflect his unconditional love and acceptance and fulfill his purpose for friendship when we reach out to others as he reaches out to them.

Jesus taught this principle while he was a guest at the home of a Pharisee. The Pharisees were legalistic religious hypocrites. They sought to dot every "i" and cross every "t" of the Jewish law. In their obsession with perfection, they excluded people who didn't measure up to their personal standards. Jesus condemned their exclusivity:

> "When you give a luncheon or dinner, do not invite your friends, your brothers or relatives, or your rich neighbors; if you do, they may invite you back and so you will be repaid. But when you give a banquet, invite the poor, the crippled, the lame, the blind, and you will be blessed. Although they cannot repay you, you will be repaid at the resurrection of the righteous."
>
> Luke 14:12–14

As my friend, John Rice, said, "A friend is one who will give of himself whenever you call for help, with no thought of reward."

Does God's plan for purposeful friendship mean that you will always be pouring yourself out into challenging relationships with "difficult" people? Does obedience to Christ mean that you will miss out on fun mutual friendships? Let's look at Jesus' example.

Jesus was always serving and ministering to the needs of people around him. As I read through the New Testament, I am amazed at his grueling schedule. Jesus spent most of his time with society's most unlovable people—the "down and outers." Did Jesus have time for any close friends?

Yes! Remember that Jesus operated in concentric circles of friends—the crowds of people, the disciples following him, the apostles whom he had called, and the threesome, Peter, James and John. Obeying Jesus' example, we are called to reach out to "the crowds"—those whom the world rejects. We are called to interact with even the most unwanted people as friends. This is the exciting part of being Jesus' friend: as we rely on our Source to extend friendship, God supplies our need for an "inner circle"—the comradery, encouragement and accountability of close friends.

I hope that you are catching the vision for purposeful friendship. These basics for living out purposeful friendship are not a "to do" list. They are meant to be an encouragement to you. Remember, God who designed friendships wants to be your Source and Supply. I am praying that you will experience the joy and fulfillment of God's plan for meaning and purpose in your friendships.

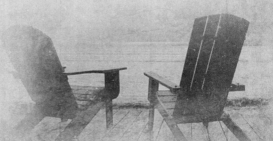

"A friend is someone that jumps higher than you when you cross the line of victory."

SAMMY TIPPIT

"We love those who know the worst of us and don't turn their faces away."

JOHN BUCHAN

A Friend to Share

"A friend loves at all times…"

PROVERBS 17:17A

"Best friend, my wellspring in the wilderness."

GEORGE ELIOT

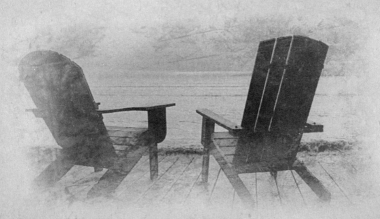

❈

This little café is wonderful! The location is perfect. The food is great, and the atmosphere couldn't be better! It is exactly the kind of place we like. I know Barb will love it. I can hardly wait to take her.

"I can't believe I got a hole-in-one playing golf with you, Ben! This is awesome! You got me my first set of clubs and inspired my love for the game. And now I get a hole-in-one playing golf with you. I will remember this day as long as I live."

My friend Paul has promised to call me when he shoots a wild turkey. When he goes hunting, I can hardly wait until he calls. The other day I knew he was in the woods on the first day of spring gobbler season. I called as soon as I thought he would be back home. I wanted to know all the details. I was excited about his day even though he did not get a bird.

There's something about sharing a moment with a friend. To be the bearer of good news, to make a friend smile—there are few joys that compare.

"We love because . . ."
∞

God is the author of friendship. He designed friends to be more than social companions who pass easily into and out of our lives. Since creation, he has been showing his loving-kindness, getting into the thick of human trials and delights. Though God may allow difficulties in our lives, the pages of the Bible make it clear that he is never distant or indifferent. God loves people. As the "weeping prophet" Jeremiah wrote, "Since ancient times no one has heard, no ear has perceived, no eye has seen any God besides you, who acts on behalf of those who wait for him" (Jeremiah 64:4). From the beginning of time, God has been involved with humanity. But sending his only Son, Jesus, to live and die for us was God's most radical overture of friendship.

As "God with us," Jesus raised the bar. He cast a new vision for friendship. Our lives are not meant to be compartmentalized between religion, social interaction, and personal needs. Jesus came down to earth to be our Friend and Lord. Jesus' sacrificial death and resurrection bridged the chasm of sin separating us from a holy God. Jesus is evidence that God desires to have an intimate relationship with us; a relationship that fundamentally changes the way we see ourselves and interact with our friends.

God says the stakes are high in the ways we conduct our friendships:

We love because he first loved us. If anyone says, "I love God," yet hates his brother, he is a liar. For anyone who does not love his brother, whom he has seen, cannot love God, whom he has not seen. And he has given us this command: Whoever loves God must also love his brother.

1 John 4:19–21

Leave it to the apostle John to bring a spiritual truth into the practicalities of everyday life. He's saying, *"If I can't love the friend I meet for lunch, how can I love God whom I've never seen?"* Your expressions of love—sacrificial, enduring, patient, genuine love—to your friends reflects the extent of your love for God, who loves you sacrificially, enduringly, patiently, genuinely.

Our Friend and Lord Jesus is intimately involved in even the most casual of our friendships. That's the beauty and joy of friendship with Jesus. He is the Source and Supply. Remember his assurance, "I am the vine; you are the branches. If a man remains in me and I in him, he will bear much fruit; apart from me you can do noth- ing" (John 15:4–5). While we are called to love our friends as evidence of our love for

God, we're not expected to do it on our own determination and strength. Jesus is there to love our friends through us, one day at a time.

My friend, John Dresher, tells the story of his daughter who became frightened during a thunderstorm. She ran to her dad crying and climbed up onto his lap. As any good dad would do, John tried to console his crying daughter. As he comforted her, he said, "Honey, you don't need to be frightened. God loves you!" Her response speaks volumes: "Daddy, I know God loves me, but right now I want someone to love me with skin on."

That is a wonderful definition of friendship: being "God's love with skin on."

Pass it on

Jesus' kind of friendship is something to be passed on. Jesus was always reaching out and sending out. With our personal security based in his love and care for us, we can also reach out with abandon. You no longer have to hedge your bets, making careful calculations and reading between the lines to protect yourself. With God's strength and wisdom as your Source and Supply, you are finally free to be a friend.

Let's return once more to the two most important commands in life. Jesus said: 1. "'Love the Lord your God with all your heart and with all your soul and with all your mind and with all your strength.'" 2. "'Love your neighbor as yourself'"

(Mark 12:30–31). By pairing love for God with love for your neighbor, Jesus shows that loving God is to be the cornerstone and impetus of our human interaction. Friendship and relationship with God are meant to be shared.

The acts of friendship are all about "passing on," not limiting relationship to a choice few. We are called to demonstrate commitment, refusing to be "fair-weather friends." Sharing in friendship is to include our joys and sorrows, experiences and resources. Kindness is modeled for us by God's quickness to forgive and restore. Encouragement is one of the traits of friendship that so richly sweetens life. Availability and confidentiality build the trust a friendship needs to thrive. Sacrifice is a distinctive of the kind of relationships Jesus calls us to live. Touch is an important way of showing our personal concern and reflecting the way Jesus lived among us, reaching out in care, healing and acceptance.

In the inevitable challenges of friendship, Jesus calls us to extend love and restoration above our desires to avoid the issue, "dump" the friend, or get even. As the apostle Paul learned the hard way, even in the midst of disagreement, love "is not easily angered" and "keeps no record of wrongs" (1 Corinthians 13:5). Busyness, perhaps the most "benign" challenge a friendship can face, is met with Jesus' example to

value friends as a trust, above tasks and obligations. In the midst of pain, it is a comfort to know that we cannot face a struggle or temptation which Jesus has not experienced during his years on earth. This is especially true of the searing pain of betrayal. We aren't left to figure out responses to our struggles with friendship. The Bible outlines proven principles of tough love, accountability, forgiveness and restoration.

Keeping it simple

Fishing instructor Jim Grassi writes of fellow fisherman Bill Reinhart's first boyhood fishing trip in *Promising Waters: Stories of Fishing and Following Jesus*. Bill's father was serving in the Korean War and wasn't around to show his son the ropes. But a kind sporting goods clerk worked with Bill's limited funds and set him up with a simple wooden pole. Along the makeshift fishing rod, he was outfitted with a line of green string with a small hook and weight dangling at the end.

The clerk assured Bill that he had everything he needed. He then instructed the boy on where to find the best fishing spot and how to use the best techniques in casting his line. When Bill hiked down to the private lake where he and his mother were camping, he found dozens of experienced fishermen with their expensive gear casting far out into the lake. On Bill's first awkward cast, only a few feet into the lake, he reeled in a 10–inch bass. Immediately, he was the envy of the other fishermen.

Reinhart says, "I'm not sure what the moral to the story is, but it seems to me that sometimes we miss opportunities close by, by looking too far." Sometimes we make friendship bigger and more intimidating than it really is. Always remember it's simply being "God's love with skin on." God, your Source and Supply, has chosen to love people through you.

Jesus, our Redeemer Friend, teaches us how to fish—to reach out to others with the kind of friendship that he has shown us. He said, "Follow me and I will make you fishers of men." He shows us the best fishing spots, opening our eyes to the people who need a touch of purposeful friendship. He said, "Look at the fields! They are ripe for harvest" (John 4:35b). He teaches us about technique, demonstrating how to express his love and compassion through our lives. He said, "If anyone gives even a cup of cold water to one of these little ones because he is my disciple, I tell you the truth, he will certainly not loose his reward" (Matthew 10:42).

Jesus with us

Jesus taught us how to fish. He has even shown us the best fishing spots. But he goes a step farther: Jesus joins us for the expedition. He came to the place where we

were camping to "dwell" with us. The apostle John writes that Jesus, God's Word, "became flesh and made his dwelling among us . . ." (John 1:14). The Greek word, "skênoo" translated "dwelled" is the verb form of the word for "tabernacle," as if to say Jesus pitches a tent alongside our tent. In this journey of life, a tent is a good metaphor for his presence with us.

Pastor David Jeremiah writes in his book *A Bend in the Road*:

There can be no greater geometric line than the one defined by the distance between those two points—my lowliness and his omnipotent perfection. And yet he is "with me." That word *emanu*—"with me"—travels through time and becomes something deeper and wiser, just as all of us hopefully do. *Emanu* ultimately gives birth to a new word, *Emmanuel*: "God with us."

What will it be like to have Jesus "with you" as you interact with friends and strangers today? I believe that God has divine appointments arranged for you. As I share two stories from my life, I pray that God will open your eyes to the special moments he has planned for you. When that "neighbor" crosses your path, ask God to be your Source and Supply. He can give you courage and wisdom to step out in purposeful friendship.

I can still remember the way I felt as Ed bowed his head on the golf course and asked Jesus to forgive his sin and become Lord of his life. Ed and I had gone to high school together. My dad was his pastor. At that point in our lives, neither of us knew Christ as Savior and Lord. After high school, we lost touch with each other. I became a believer and a pastor. Ed became a successful businessman and got transferred by his company to the city where I was serving as pastor.

In the providence of God, the local newspaper featured a story about the church that I was serving. Ed was lying on the floor of his family room on a Sunday morning when he saw the article. He called to Lea, his wife and said, "You aren't going to believe this, but Steve Wingfield is a pastor!" He then said to himself, "If God can help him, maybe he can help me."

The next week Ed and Lea were in church. He called me a few days later and asked me to play golf with him. I told him I was not a good golfer, but I would enjoy going to be with him. I still rejoice over what God did at Countryside Golf Club in Roanoke, Virginia. Ed made the most important decision of his life. I believe one cannot know true joy until you have prayed with a friend who is receiving Christ as Savior and Lord. By the way, God called Ed out of the business world. He went back to college and then to seminary. For several years, we had the privilege of ministering together. He now serves as senior pastor of a growing church in Illinois. God is good!

Recently, my wife Barbara and I were in Hawaii visiting our

daughter Michelle, her husband Howard, and our new grandson, Phin. (Check out "Phinehas" in Numbers 25:11–13.) I was sitting at the local Starbucks one morning, enjoying a cup of coffee and making phone calls.

The man at the next table noticed my golf hat and asked, "Do you play golf?" We had a brief conversation, and he then asked, "Would you like to join me and two of my friends for a round of golf this afternoon?" I called home to check with Barbara, and she agreed that I should accept the invitation. I had always wanted to play golf in Hawaii, and this was my chance. I biked back to Michelle and Howard's home where my new friend, Kimo, and his two friends picked me up.

It was a picture-perfect island day and we were enjoying the golf game when I discovered that two of my new friends were battling alcoholism. They were about 30 days into a recovery program. At an appropriate time, I told Phil I would be praying for him to discover Jesus as the true "Higher Power" because Jesus could give him victory over his battle with alcohol.

Later one of the men asked what I do, and I said, "I am a minister of the Gospel." That led to several other questions. When we finished our round of golf and were driving home, Kimo asked, "Steve what caused you to want to be a minister?" I took the opportunity to share my story with the three men. When we arrived at Michelle and Howard's home, I asked if it would be okay to pray before saying goodbye. They all said they would appreciate me praying for them. I prayed briefly, thanking God for a beautiful day spent with three new friends. I asked God to continue speaking to each of them and prayed they would all come to know Christ in a personal way. They thanked me for the prayer, and I thanked them for a great day on the golf course.

The next morning I biked to Starbucks again. When I turned on my cell phone, I had a message. It was from Kimo and had been sent at 1 A.M. He said, "Steve, I can't sleep. God is dealing with me. I need to talk to you." I called him at once. "Kimo, I'm back in Kailua, at Starbucks. Where are you?" I asked.

"I will be there in five minutes," he replied.

When he walked into Starbucks, Kimo was ready to pray. I explained the gospel, and he gave his life to Christ in what he and I now call "Starbucks Chapel."

After praying together, I began to do some "follow-up." I discovered that Kimo did not have a Bible. I had seen a Christian bookstore in town, so I threw my bike in the back of Kimo's SUV and we drove to the bookstore. In the bookstore, I chose a *Life Application Study Bible* for him and began to show him some verses. Revelation 12:11 talks about overcoming the devil through your testimony (your story). After I explained the verse to him, I told Kimo, "You should tell everyone in the store what just happened to you."

I love people who have just discovered the joy of knowing Jesus! Kimo's first response was, "If it will help me be an overcomer, let's do it!" I got the attention of the shoppers and the clerks and said, "My friend has something he wants to tell you." Kimo said, "I just asked the Lord Jesus to forgive all my sins and to come live in my heart." Everyone celebrated his decision and thanked him for his boldness. It was a great encouragement for all.

We left the bookstore and returned home where I introduced Kimo to Barbara and Michelle. He and I spent another hour together going over the Bible and how to use it. We agreed to meet the next day at Starbucks Chapel at 9 A.M. for coffee and Bible study.

The next morning, I arrived a few minutes early. I noticed two men studying the Bible. I went over to their table and introduced myself. I discovered that one of the men is a local pastor. I told him about Kimo and his decision to follow Christ. I said, "Before you leave, please stop by our table and I will introduce you." I added, "Kimo is going to need lots of encouragement because he is a recovering alcoholic." The other man at the table said, "Praise God! I am in charge of our church's Christian recovery program."

God directs the steps of the righteous. There are no accidents, only divine appointments! Kimo was baptized on Easter Sunday in the Pacific Ocean. The following Sunday, he told his story to the entire church. Since then, Kimo has called me on several Saturdays from Starbucks Chapel. As he says, "God is all over Starbucks, man!"

If you pray and make yourself available, God will open doors of opportunity for you in new and existing friendships. God loves to work through our friendships. He invented friends! He wants to live in an intimate relationship with you. He wants to fulfill your deepest needs and desires for a friend. I cannot tell you how many friends you will have or who they will be, but I know one thing for certain. God has good purposes and divine appointments in store for your friendships.

> *"In ones' walk with the Lord, if you have five friends that will walk with you, you are a blessed man."*
>
> RICKY SKAGGS

> *"Reflect that life, like every other blessing, derives its value from its use alone. Similarly, friendship derives its merit from the intangibles of delectation."*
>
> SAMUEL JOHNSON

Friendship, the Verb

"If a friend is in trouble, don't annoy him by asking if there is anything you can do. Think up something appropriate and do it."

Edgar Watson Howe

"Friendship should have feet."

Ralph Waldo Emerson

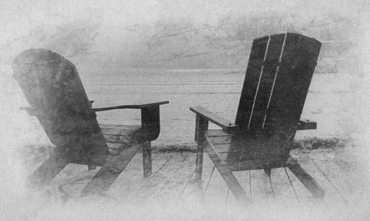

Have you ever noticed that many of the words we commonly associate with affection can be used as either a noun (a "thing") or a verb (an "action")? Embrace, kiss, love, touch, hug, care . . . these words function both as nouns and as verbs. I can give *an embrace*. Or I can *embrace*. I may both have *a true love* and *love* her. You can undoubtedly think of other examples.

According to most standard dictionaries, the word "friendship" is only a noun. However, the Oxford English Dictionary notes an archaic and rare use of "friendship" as a verb. Our word "friend" is derived from the Anglo-Saxon "freond" which had its roots in a verb meaning "to love." In its earliest definitions, it meant "to praise, trust or believe." B. Long may have been speaking more literally than she imagined when she said, "friendship is a verb."

Centuries before Long or the English word "friend" existed, Jesus had already redefined friendship. In the greatest action ever taken, God arrived on earth in person. Jesus, "God with us," said to his disciples, "I have called you friends . . ." (John

15:15). God initiated friendship, and I pray that Jesus' example lived out across the pages of the Bible has personally redefined friendship for you.

Friendship is an action. It entails so much more than the casual social contacts people pursue to stave off loneliness. God designed human relationships to be purposeful, growing, challenging, fulfilling. It breaks my heart to see people settling for less. God has a better plan for friendship!

I've glimpsed that plan in my own life and the experience has left me wanting more. I still have much to learn about being a friend, but I have clearly seen God's hand working through my friends to impact me. When God is moving in our friendships, they are an incredible source of fun, accountability, support and encouragement.

You are not meant to go through life alone. Friendships are one of your best opportunities to be sharpened and to mature as a person. They are also one of your best avenues to make a lasting impact in life.

Today more than ever in western culture there is a desperate need for active friendship. In *Radical Acts of Love*, author Susan Skog tells of touring the United States extensively to promote an earlier book she had written on depression. She asked every audience the same question: "How many of you have enough supportive family and friends?" In five years, she never saw more than one-fourth of the hands raised.

Dr. Redford Williams, Director of the Behavioral Medical

Research Center at Duke University, conducted a five-year study of 1,000 heart disease patients. In an interview recorded in Marla Paul's book, *The Friendship Crisis*, Williams reports an amazing connection between friendship and recovery. As expected, married patients survived longer than unmarried ones. However, Williams was surprised to find that unmarried patients who had a close friend or confidante had a much higher survival rate (85%) than those without one (50%). In fact, single patients with a close friend had the same survival rate as patients with a spouse. God gave us friendship to bring value and purpose to our lives.

The great 20th Century theologian Francis Schaeffer said, "We must all measure ourselves by our friendships. Apart from the Scriptures, there is no surer measure to be had in this poor fallen world."

How are your friendships today? Are they in need of maintenance or repair? Are they thriving and challenging? Have you caught the vision for taking your casual friendships a step deeper? Do you have a plan to bring purpose into your everyday interactions?

God has a plan for your friendships. With his help, I challenge you to make friendship a verb—an intentional act every day for the rest of your life.

"Friends who live in the Lord never see each other for the last time."

MARK & MARTHA YODER

"A true friend unbosoms freely, advises justly, assists readily, adventures boldly, takes all patiently, defends courageously, and continues a friend unchangeably."

WILLIAM PENN